ABOUT THE AUTHOR

When Earl Ofari wrote *The Myth of Black Capitalism*, he was just twenty-three, married, and held a degree in psychology from California State College in L.A., where he was instrumental in setting up one of North America's first Black student unions. At the time, he had already appeared in such publications as the *Guardian* and *Los Angeles Free Press*, and had crafted pamphlets for the Radical Education Project. Since then he has written extensively on race and politics for the *Los Angeles Times*, *Newsday*, the *Washington Post*, the *Christian Science Monitor*, the *Chicago Tribune*, and the *Baltimore Sun*. He holds an MA from California State University Dominguez Hills. He has been a frequent guest on CNN and MSNBC and co-hosted the Al Sharpton Show for nearly a decade. Hutchinson hosts the live call-in program *The Earl Ofari Hutchinson Show* on Pacifica Radio and is a nationally acclaimed author and social issues commentator.

The Myth of Black Capitalism

NEW EDITION

by EARL OFARI HUTCHINSON

MONTHLY REVIEW PRESS

New York

Second edition copyright © 2023 Monthly Review Press
Original edition copyright © 1970 Monthly Review Press

All Rights Reserved

Library of Congress Cataloging-in-Publication data
available from the publisher

ISBN paper: 978-1-68590-031-1
ISBN cloth: 978-1-68590-032-8

Typeset in Bulmer MT

MONTHLY REVIEW PRESS, NEW YORK
monthlyreview.org

5 4 3 2 1

Contents

Is Black Capitalism Still a Myth?

The year was 1968. Then Republican presidential candidate Richard Nixon was in the midst of an intense dogfight with Democratic presidential nominee and the vice president Hubert Humphrey for the White House. Nixon needed an edge.

The edge was the race card. He covered two of his political flanks playing it. One was his so-called Southern Strategy. Put simply that meant saying little and doing even less on the fight for racial equity that would rile the white conservative South.

The second was to come up with something, anything that would dent the ironclad lock the Democrats had on the Black vote. This meant he had to appear that he was not the polarizing racist that many Blacks regarded him and the GOP as. His idea was crass and cynical, but in one sense it was brilliant.

He combined two words that appeared on the surface to be an oxymoron. They were "Black" and "Capitalism." This wasn't just a con man's eye-catching sloganeering. Nixon sought to put body behind it. In his acceptance speech at the 1968 GOP presidential convention, he thundered, "Let government use its tax and credit policies to enlist in this battle the greatest engine of progress ever developed in the history of man—American private enterprise."

In the immediate months after, Nixon trotted out a parade of prominent African American sports, entertainment, and business entrepreneurs to gush over his Black Capitalism call and, of course, endorse his candidacy.

This touched off a fierce debate among African Americans that essentially boiled down to two questions: Could Blacks really be capitalists? How could Blacks attain some measure of economic independence, wealth building, and most important, business and financial ownership?

In 1968, I was a graduate student, president of the campus Black Student Union, and, as were many young Blacks, a radical, the label in vogue before "activist" and "progressive" supplanted it. I, and others, were deeply enthralled by Marx and Marxism. The Nixon call stirred a mix of fascination, awe, and anger. It also stirred a burning desire to dig deep into the history of Black economic development and in the process debunk it.

The result was *The Myth of Black Capitalism*. In the introduction, I laid down the gauntlet: "Future programs for black liberation definitely should not include capitalism in any form." I fleshed out a hard-nosed radical critique of Black Capitalism and lambasted those I termed the "Black Elite" for trying to foster what I considered this fraud on Blacks.

But there are two often daunting facts of life. One is that things change, while at the same time they stay the same. That holds true for politics, people, and often one's point of view. That is, in one's thinking about events and issues over time.

In the half-century since the initial publication of my book, successive presidents up to and including Biden and even Trump all borrowed a page from Nixon's Black Capitalism playbook in their pitches to Blacks. They pledged to provide more funding, support, programs, and technical assistance to minority businesses.

In the same period, some Blacks have often, with much media fanfare, become major sports team owners, corporate, bank, and

Wall Street firm CEOs, and major investors in and owners of an array of varied business enterprises.

To many, this seemed irrefutable proof that Blacks not only can be capitalists but *are* capitalists. There's also the side-by-side debate over the new buzzwords—Black financial empowerment, wealth building, financial and business literacy, financial planning and management, and debt avoidance. These phrases have struck a deep chord among many African Americans. They have engendered healthy debate and discussion, striking to the heart of the need for prudent financial solvency and security.

However, a half-century after my book's release, one thing hasn't changed, and that is the brutal reality that still firmly bolsters my initial critique. Blacks are still entrenched at or near the bottom of the economic ladder. They consistently in the past fifty years have had the highest rate of joblessness, and poverty, and the lowest rate of business ownership. They remain mired at the bottom of America's economic and financial ladder.

A 2019 NBC study found that Blacks represent less than one percentage point (0.8 percent) of *Fortune* 500 CEOs. The number is even more damning when one considers that Blacks make up 10 percent of college graduates. Proportionately, Blacks then should make up at least fifty Black CEOs. There were only four at the time.

In 2020, Blacks owned less than 3 percent of American businesses. Even this was misleading. The bulk of them were still mom-and-pop sole proprietorships, with one or two employees.

The COVID pandemic revealed another deflating fact about Black business ownership. That's how tenuous and fragile it is.

This figure was oft cited after Trump and Congress passed the COVID stimulus relief packages in 2020. Ninety percent of minority businesses did not get a nickel of money from the SBA's Payroll Protection Program. For Black-owned businesses, the number was even worse. Ninety percent got no funding.

In several informal polls on my *Facebook* pages during the pandemic, I asked the same question: "Do you know of any

Black-owned business that got a COVID stimulus SBA Payroll Protection Program Loan?" There were a handful of "yes's." There was an avalanche of "no's." Some expressed optimism that the grim shutoff of the money spigot to Black businesses might change with the House passage of an added $3 trillion stimulus package. However, the hope was guarded and cautious.

At first glance, the abysmally low numbers seemed ridiculous. Trump, congressional leaders, and Treasury officials loudly pledged that small businesses were a prime target of the aid program. There was a litany of much publicized online workshops and town halls on where and how to apply for funding. Many banks announced that they had funds and encouraged businesses to apply. House Democrats sweetened the pot by prying $60 billion out of the loan package for minority banks. Yet, the low number of Black businesspersons who got money never budged.

There was much justified finger-pointing at the SBA, Treasury officials, corporate and bank lobbyists for lax to nonexistent oversight, lax rules on who could get the money, and for earmarking far too much of the half trillion in business loans to major corporations.

There was equally justified finger-pointing at the banks for tossing up a mountain of paperwork, tax and business filing documents, and account requirements that small business owners had little chance of hurdling. Then there was the muddle, confusion, and constant changing edicts about what and how the money could be used and what if any of it had to be paid back.

Little had changed except the desperation of countless numbers of near penniless, distressed Black small business owners. The clock ticked on the future survival of Black businesses. There was no guarantee that the businesses would reopen their doors, and when they did, that their customers would be back. Many closed their doors permanently.

Making government funds immediately available for Black-owned businesses was then and always vital to counter the inherent ideological and structural tilt toward the big corporations that is built into all government contracting, taxing, and endless subsidies that is the virtual sole province of corporate America. For instance, during the pandemic, Wells Fargo flatly said in a memo that it "prioritized" loans to its biggest and supposedly best customers, namely the major firms. It took much heat for its candor and in quick damage control said it would donate the hefty lending fees it raked into non-profits. At least that is what it said.

Black businesses have long been a specially endangered breed when it came to getting a dime out of banks and the government. The reasons are well documented: the lack of credit, a proven business track record, resources, expertise, and a long-standing cozy business connection and relationship with the banks. Then there is the dizzying gauntlet of wage and tax forms, documents, and filings needed to qualify for a loan. Much of the work is done online and that means having a computer, computer access, and computer skills to go through the cyber paperwork required.

Countless surveys by business groups, federal regulators, and watchdog groups have produced reams of figures to show that despite the PR lip service lenders pay to wanting to loan to small businesses, the paltry number of loans they make annually to small, and especially minority, businesses has remained frozen over past decades.

On the plus side, Black businesses, I'll concede, have been a needed engine for employment, wealth building, financial security, and, importantly, hope for many Blacks. They have served as showpieces for Black financial and economic achievement and independence. They have spurred generations to pursue the oft-touted American dream of entrepreneurship and the means to be your own boss.

Yet a half-century plus after the publication of *The Myth of Black Capitalism* the state of Black business remains exactly as I wrote in 1970—small, and marginalized. Today, as then, it cannot be said that they are the embodiment of the capitalism that Nixon proclaimed as his goal for Blacks in 1968. In short, as I wrote in 1970, Black Capitalism is still a myth.

You show me a capitalist, I'll show you a bloodsucker. He cannot be anything but a bloodsucker if he's going to be a capitalist. He's got to get it from somewhere other than himself, and that's where he gets it—from somewhere or someone other than himself.

—MALCOLM X

As Long as the Man controls the water or electricity coming into your community, it does you no good to control that community. And to control the community in a capitalistic way, like the Man, is not desirable.

—H. RAP BROWN

The mode of production in material life determines the general character of the social, political, and spiritual processes of life.

—KARL MARX

Introduction to the First Edition

Black investigators have, from time to time, been forced to deal with various aspects of "black" business and the possibility of an independent black economy. The most prominent of these investigators, black sociologist E. Franklin Frazier, came to the conclusion that "black" business was a myth. Frazier, in his seminal work *Black Bourgeoisie,* went on to give an extended analysis of the historic trends that have led to the current enthusiasm for black business and its embrace by black leaders. As Frazier has written regarding these black leaders: "The myth of Negro business is tied up with the belief in the possibility of a separate Negro economy. . . . Of course, behind the idea of the separate Negro economy is the hope of the black bourgeoisie that they will have the monopoly of the Negro market."[1]

Frazier, like his contemporaries, did not go far enough in his conclusion, primarily because he was himself so very much a part of the black elite. This imposed limitations on his willingness to expose the real roots of the failure of black business. Consequently, the conclusions he did come to tended to sidetrack the reasons for black business failure and ignore the existence of a vested-interest class—the "black bourgeoisie." Frazier did not really consider the effects of corporate capitalism's economic domination; instead he chose to concentrate on its more peripheral manifestations in white racism, lack of education on the part of black people, and so on.

The call for black capitalism today by the descendants of Frazier's black bourgeoisie—the black elite—is more than just a rekindling of a misdirected faith in the myth of Negro business. It is part of a thorough black exercise in mass self-delusion. Behind it all lies a legacy of misleadership historically constructed by the American system.

The entire issue could have been avoided by an objective view, by the black leadership, of the functional character of American capitalism. A thorough understanding of the working dynamic of capitalism is absolutely necessary for black people today if they are to grasp properly its relationship to black America.

Black people have the weakest commercial tradition of any people in the United States. For historical reasons, including alienation from the capitalist system and from their African communal tradition, they have been little attracted to trade, shopkeeping, buying and selling, or employing labor for the purpose of exploitation. Thus the tradition of black capitalism discussed in these pages is very weak and is confined, for the most part, to a small black elite. This elite has, when politically active, pressed black capitalism upon the black masses as a program to solve their problems, but never with significant results. The black masses have rarely shown an interest in black capitalism as a solution. It is this record of failure which is documented in this book, in the hope that it will help the black people to put the present cries for "black capitalism" in their proper perspective and reject them once again.

Future programs for black liberation definitely should not include capitalism in any form. This means, of course, that both white capitalism in practice and black capitalism in theory and in hope must be destroyed.

1

The Origin of the Legacy

W. E. B. Du Bois has written: "Yet on the west coast [of Africa] was perhaps the greatest attempt in human history before the twentieth century to build a culture based on peace and beauty, to establish a Communism of industry and of distribution of goods and services according to need."[1]

The observation by Dr. Du Bois on African communalism presents a striking contrast to the current call for black capitalism. In every respect, capitalism runs counter to the fundamental ethic which for centuries provided the base for African society.

Modern capitalism was in fact an essentially foreign import to the African continent. The traditional cultural, social, and economic foundations of African tribal society were squarely rooted in a very ancient form of communalism.

This system had been preserved and passed on intact through many generations. Before the European colonial onslaught, communalism had been developed to a very high level. Basic necessities of life such as food, shelter, and even clothing were shared. Much of a tribe's land and property were held in common. Often it was simply distributed equally among the tribe's various members.

From this early cooperative sharing, a pattern developed which facilitated acceptance by all in the tribe of a common value system. This in turn gave a unique character to all African social attitudes, and the cohesion necessary to hold the society together as a solidified, collective unit was developed.

Melville J. Herskovits discusses this particular aspect of African society at great length. He has even shown how many of the characteristics of tribal economic collectivism have carried over to areas of the United States where black people predominate. In fact, he ascribes all cooperative and mutual aid efforts among black people to the strict tradition "of [African] discipline and control based on acquiescence and directed toward the furtherance of community needs."[2] Herskovits concludes: "The tradition of cooperation in the field of economic endeavor is outstanding in Negro cultures everywhere."

The mass intrusion of the colonial nations into Africa in the sixteenth century drastically changed this pattern. The traditional African cultural-economic system was completely shattered. With the subsequent advent of the slave trade, Africa was literally stripped of its values and institutions. This, of course, included its whole communal framework.

The few black people in America to receive their freedom before the emancipation act of the Civil War were caught in a double dilemma. On the one hand, the years they had spent in slavery had left them with no knowledge of the former cultural methods and techniques of the communal systems of Africa. On the other, they had no real understanding of the intricacies of American capitalism. Chattel slavery, the most brutal and extreme form of capitalism, had readied the minds of its black vassals for the future misleadership of the black masses.

Despite the lack of background or training in business or economics, a few "free" black people attempted to set up businesses in the small scattered black communities of the North. The earliest ventures in the field were marked with an occasional success. This could be attributed largely to the black people's tendency, born of the necessity to survive, to pool their meager financial resources.

Although racism was even then an all-powerful factor in American life, it should theoretically have been easier in the eighteenth century for black people to achieve success in business than it is today. Eighteenth-century America was still largely an unsettled land, and the country's economy was basically rural-agrarian. Capitalism was in a very infantile stage of development.

Inspired by what some black people perceived to be success, "mutual aid" societies were established in a few black communities. The early black entrepreneurs recognized that if they were to attain any success in developing black businesses to an appreciable level in the black community, it would come only through economic cooperation.

It was quite apparent to them that no concrete help in obtaining capital and credit could be expected from white America.

The milestone in organizing came with the establishment of the Free African Society in Philadelphia in 1787, by two of the black community's leaders, Absalom Jones and Richard Allen. The Free African Society existed for the stated purpose of promoting "cooperative aid" among black people. Here, for the first time, an organized leadership had developed in the black community. Significantly, it grew up around the issue of the community's economic survival. Out of this tiny nucleus of self-appointed black leaders emerged a weak but noticeable black elite.

Upon examination of the Society's financial rules, the significance of this elite becomes clearer. It was stipulated that each black person in Philadelphia should contribute one silver shilling a month to the Society. Supposedly, after one year, part of the money collected would be distributed to the city's poor and needy blacks. The funds were to be handled by a *select* committee of the Society's members whose task it was "to dispose of money in hand to the best advantage and use of the Society."

The following years saw a succession of other mutual aid societies spring up in many northern and some southern cities where

sizeable black populations existed. By 1813 there were eleven
benevolent societies of this kind in Philadelphia alone. By 1838,
this number had increased to one hundred, with a membership
of 7,448. The members of the societies paid in $18,851 and
received $14,172 in benefits.[3]

The newly emergent black elite's economic interests soon predominated over those of the black masses. The black elite began
exploring the possibilities of expanding their activities into other
areas. The more far-sighted among them recognized even at this
early date that the segregated isolation in which black people
were forced to exist could be beneficial to their personal economic designs.

In the early eighteenth century many of the black communities in the North had already achieved some measure of social
stability. The logical area of economic concentration was the field
of real estate and housing. The black elite had, in fact, already
begun to accumulate substantial resources in this area.

Before the end of the eighteenth century, the black elite had
property holdings totaling $250,000. By 1847 this figure had
increased to $400,000. In 1856, the black elite in Philadelphia
reached its pre–Civil War economic apex, with real estate holdings valued at nearly $1 million.[4]

The small black elite that existed at the time unquestionably
held the bulk of the black communities' economic power. In
Philadelphia, for example, it was estimated that less than 6 percent of the black community in the city proper actually owned
any property.[5]

Dr. Du Bois, in his detailed study of Philadelphia's black community in the nineteenth century, recognized the inadequacy of
the approach which the black elite presented to the black community. He writes:

> These attempts [to develop black business] would, however, be
> vastly more successful in another economic age. Today, as before
> noted, the application of large capital to the retail business, the

gathering of workmen into factories, the wonderful success of trained talent in catering to the whims and taste of customers almost precludes the effective competition of the small store.[6]

With this, Dr. Du Bois clearly dismisses as already outdated the trivial efforts of the black elite to develop businesses. At this time a few blacks began to look to Africa for their business pursuits. Paul Cuffe is perhaps one of the best examples. In 1775, Cuffe, sixteen years of age, signed on to the crew of a New England whaling vessel. The experience he gained at sea he soon put to use. He acquired several ships and went into the transport business. Cuffe was successful, and in the following years he was able to expand his operation. By 1806 he had a private fleet numbering some five or six ships. Cuffe then turned his attention to West Africa, where he sought to develop a black economic base through private commerce. As a result of his voyages to Africa, he conceived the idea of recolonizing American blacks in Africa. In 1815 he was able to transport several thousand blacks from America to Africa for settlement.

Cuffe's commercial success, coupled with his African colonization venture, made him one of the richest black men in America. Unfortunately, his ideal of black economic development, however nobly conceived, coincided with many of the goals of the tiny black-elite merchant class that prospered during and immediately after the Revolutionary War. Even more, Cuffe's excursions into Africa set the precedent for the later African colonization plans of many prospective nineteenth-century black businessmen.

During this same period, the system of chattel slavery in the Bourbon South had reached its pinnacle of power. In emulation of the planter-aristocrats, a few free black people sought to exploit this system for their own personal gain. It has been estimated that in 1830 there were 3,777 black slave masters in the United States.[7] How many of these black masters bought slaves in order to emancipate them is not known. This has led to much speculation and controversy. Eugene Boykin has pointed out that "many purchased slaves for purposes of liberation, but many others hired slaves for profit." Boykin further states: "In Louisiana there was a large number of wealthy colored families, many of whom owned plantations and slaves. . . . Nowhere in America was there a black planter aristocracy comparable."[8]

It would probably be fair to conclude that the majority of the free blacks who purchased slaves did so out of humanitarian considerations. In his study of the history of the black people, *From Slavery to Freedom,* John Hope Franklin notes:

> Frequently the husband purchased his wife or vice versa; or the slaves were the children of a free father who had purchased his wife; or they were other relatives or friends who had been rescued from the worst features of the institution by some affluent free Negro.

However, in many cases this was not true. As Franklin goes on to relate: "There were instances, however, in which free Negroes had a real economic interest in the institution of slavery and held slaves in order to improve their economic status."

This latter fact should not be very difficult to envision, particularly in light of the existent Southern racial-economic pattern. Plantation life was viewed by a few hand-picked black people as being a quite noble experience. It provided the white planters with many creature comforts, such as little physical exertion, leisure, pleasure, and above all fantastic unearned profit. Black captive labor then provided all this plus the brutally unique self-satisfaction the Southern white planters gained from the vantage position they held in the master-slave axis.

Thus some black men, upon their emancipation, accumulated money to purchase slaves. With this, black capitalism moved into what was perhaps its most odious phase in the history of black America.

Indications of the financial benefits that these black-elite slave masters gained from the practice could be seen in places other than Louisiana. The black masters of Somerset County, Maryland, for example, were assessed on their slave property, which was valued at $4,600 in 1841 and $3,450 in 1860.[9]

The legislative bodies of various Southern states, along with the white planters, quite naturally frowned upon the idea of black people owning slaves. However, as long as black possession of slaves posed no immediate economic threat to white interests, it was tolerated and little action was taken. In fact, it was recorded that a few black masters even profited from the slave purchase provisions of the District of Columbia's emancipation act, which was passed in 1863. One former black master received $2,168.10 from the government for ten slaves, while another received $832.20 for two slaves, and still another $547.50 for one.[10]

The early nineteenth century saw this emergent black elite begin to assume a predominant position of leadership in black America. Dr. Martin R. Delaney, a Harvard-trained physician, emerged as one of the strongest leaders of the black elite. Dr. Delaney's program for the economic uplift of black America was highly tinged with the capitalist aspirations shared by Northern white merchants and speculators.

The main points of the theoretical program offered by Delaney were outlined in his book *The Condition, Elevation, Emigration, and Destiny of the Colored People of the United States, Politically Considered.* In it Delaney wrote: "Let our young men and women prepare themselves for usefulness, trading and other things of importance.... Educate them for the store and the country house ... to do everyday practical business." This, in essence, was the general sentiment prevalent among the black elite at that time.

Dr. Delaney also felt that a promising avenue for economic "progress" would lie in exploiting some of the land and mineral wealth of East Africa. The effect of such an undertaking, if practically possible, would have been to advance black capitalism into the international arena. Dr. Delaney was very aware that the program he called for would directly place the black elite in competition with the major European colonial powers.

Delaney proposed further in his book that a "confidential council" be convened, with the intended purpose of forming a Board of Commissioners. According to Delaney, this Board would be composed of certain members "whose duty and business shall be, to go on an expedition to the Eastern Coast of Africa." Nowhere in the outline of this plan did Delaney indicate any attempt on his part to solicit any support from the broad masses of free black people in the North.

His intentions became clearer when he further proposed: "The National Council shall appoint one or two special commissioners, to England [and] France, to solicit . . . the necessary outfit and support." Delaney went on to suggest that England and France, by going into partnership with the black elite, could expand the tremendous economic potential of the land and resources they already held in Africa. Delaney even couched the appeal for support he made to the black elite in the same terms used by the European profiteers: "The land is ours—there it lies with inexhaustible resources; let us go and possess it."[11]

Delaney, in calling for the support of England and France, the two recognized leaders of the imperialist powers of the nineteenth century, demonstrated the lengths to which certain elements of the black elite were prepared to go to implement this plan. From the viewpoint of Delaney and his class, it appeared that any means to secure the wealth which undoubtedly existed in East Africa was acceptable if it promised success.

Furthermore, it should be obvious that the prime motive behind Delaney's desire to include France and England in his plan stemmed from his recognition of the political-economic weakness of the black elite's position in America. By itself, the black elite could never really hope to achieve any practical gains from this venture. Even if Delaney had enlisted the support of the two countries, the precarious position of free black people in pre–Civil War America, in terms of mere physical survival, would have militated against the black elite's success.

It was also felt by some of the black elite's more knowledgeable members that Delaney's plan would not be acceptable to the tribal chiefs in Africa. It was an established fact that the numerous tribal groupings in Africa had long either occupied or reserved claims (some dating back to antiquity) to most of Africa's fertile land. This, of course, is contrary to the European-American historical lie, which has fostered the tradition that most of Africa was unexplored and uninhabited before the coming of European explorers and slave traders.

It was apparent, then, that any attempted power-grab on the part of foreigners (of any color) would be resisted by any available means. It has been thoroughly documented that numerous wars were waged by the tribes over this issue. On this point Bill McAdoo has written: "That is why [the black elite] called upon England and France to extend the necessary provisions (including military aid, of course) to accomplish their plans for possessing and exploiting Africa . . . in accordance with their Black capitalist aspirations." [12]

There is little doubt that Delaney, in particular, was well aware of these facts. At that early time, he could be considered a foremost student of African history and society. His ancestral lineage he proudly traced to West Africa.

Even more, Delaney, as the pioneer black separatist, was the guiding force behind the early black cultural nationalist movement. Delaney's writings served to give nationalism among blacks a formal ideological base. A careful reading of this material will reveal a remarkable contemporary anticipation of today's developments. For example, when Frederick Douglass in 1853 consulted Harriet Beecher Stowe (of *Uncle Tom's Cabin* fame) about a proposed educational project for black people, Delaney indignantly wrote Douglass: "She knows nothing about us . . . neither does any other white person—and, consequently can contrive no successful scheme for our elevation." Delaney went further and pointed out: "No enterprise, institution, or anything else, should be commenced for us, or our general benefit, without first consulting us."

Finally, in 1854, Delaney was able to call a convention to map out concrete plans for the implementation of his program. The convention selected two additional areas, Central America and Haiti, for possible black settlement. Delaney still held on to his original plans for East African colonization, however. While two parties left for the other of the specified areas, Delaney in 1858 left on a mission to England, for negotiations with national leaders there, and then proceeded to Africa. He finally ended up in the Niger Valley, where he signed a treaty with eight kings.

Article one of the treaty's four articles specified: That the King and Chiefs on their part, agree to grant and assign unto the said Commissioners, (in this case the members of Delaney's Niger Valley Exploring Party) on behalf of the African race in America, the right and privilege of settling in common with the Egba people, on any part of the territory belonging to Abbeokuta, not otherwise occupied.

The treaty itself simply affirmed the right of black people to emigrate to their particular territories. This quite naturally fell substantially short of Delaney's expectations.

Delaney's African venture, reexamined from a position of historical reality, was a direct, although somewhat confused, call for black economic expansion under the exclusive direction of the black elite in the classic nineteenth-century capitalist-imperialist pattern of the European nations.

Despite Delaney's failure, his message, stripped of the fantasy dream about African empires, won quick acceptance among the Northern black elite, and particularly those oriented toward business. Black capitalism became their dominant concern. From the middle to the latter part of the nineteenth century, all economic planning which involved the black elite was conducted with specific emphasis on both black business and professional development.

Toward this end, a National Negro Convention was held in Rochester, New York, in 1853, one year after the publication of Delaney's book. A large gathering assembled to work out a detailed economic program for the black masses of the North. Over one hundred delegates attended, representing the varied interests of those who composed the black elite. They laid down a series of elaborately worded articles intended to pave the way for actual black capitalist development.

Their program specifically called for such things as an organization of all branches of industry in the black communities into a "protective union for the purchase and sale of articles of domestic consumption" and a "registry of colored mechanics, artisans and business men."[13] In short, all enterprises in which the black elite were engaged were to be organized to ensure the maximum amount of economic interaction with each other. This would of course facilitate their gaining access to a wider market for their products within the black communities.

Their proposal represented, in effect, what later became known in the Northern black ghettos as a "Buy Black" campaign. This slogan was specifically coined by black merchants and businessmen in the 1920s and 1930s. "Buy Black" became a favorite tool used by the black elite to appeal to the latent nationalism within the black masses. The hope of the black elite was that this would entice black people to patronize their businesses rather than white businesses. If the black elite could eliminate white businessmen from competition with them, they would have a clear field and could step into the vacuum left by the white businesses.

Black economic viability began to share, along with social equality and slave emancipation, the attention of the black community in general. The black elite began to cultivate the idea of business solvency in their concentrated effort to expand and develop their personal economic potential in the black communities of the North. The new black leaders became more and more vociferous in their quest for both black equality and profit through capitalism.

Dr. John Rock was such a leader. Dr. Rock, a distinguished lawyer and doctor, attained one of the highest honors accorded a black man in America at that time when he became the first black lawyer accredited to practice law before the Supreme Court. Dr. Rock, as a matter of course, felt a similar leaning to that of Delaney. But Rock, unlike Delaney, was pragmatic enough to realize that it was ludicrous to expect such established colonial powers as England and France to give aid to black people in America, let alone assent to any partnership in exploitation. Rock also realized that the English and French were themselves the two nations most instrumental in expanding the African slave trade.

Nevertheless, despite Rock's sound knowledge and understanding of the historical facts and contemporary conditions of black people, the proposals he offered for black economic development were in strict conformity to those already advanced by the other spokesmen for the black elite. Consequently, in the long run, they proved just as unadaptable to the needs of black liberation. As an example, Dr. Rock was quoted in the *Liberator* of March 1858 as stating: "In this country where money is the great sympathetic nerve which ramifies society, and has a ganglia in every man's pocket, a man is respected in proportion to his success in business. When the avenues of wealth are open to us, we will then become educated and wealthy." Quite fittingly, he comes to the same naive conclusion which every leader of the black elite has come to since. "Then, and not till then, will we be able to enjoy true equality, which can exist only among peers."

In this statement, Rock exhibits a fundamental understanding of capitalism's effects. But he fails to carry his insight through to a logical conclusion: Such powerful forces as the Northern industrialists and the Southern planter-aristocrats, which controlled America, were not about to yield any of their dominance to a weak vested-interest group such as the black elite.

Rock, partly blinded by the aspirations of his class, failed in the end to provide any meaningful solutions for the economic-survival crisis facing the black masses in the North. But, with Delaney, he was influential in giving currency to the concept of black economy as the most effective means of attaining the social equality that the masses of black people then desired.

The State Convention of Ohio Colored Men was held in Cincinnati in November 1858. This convention passed a series of resolutions which gave substance to much of Rock's pronouncement. The convention went on record advising black people to think seriously about new programs designed to bring about a kind of economic system based on the principles of self-help. The programs were to be oriented toward business and industry. According to a convention resolution this would, "if everywhere established, greatly increase *our* wealth; and with it *our* power."[14]

Briefly then, the pre–Civil War period saw the trend develop in which black America began to seek its liberation through attempts at emulating the economic success which white America was enjoying through capitalist expansion. This period saw also the growth of a business-professional class, composed of black America's most educated, financially well-to-do men. This black elite sought, through numerous conferences, speeches, and meetings, to give direction to the struggle for survival in which the black masses were engaged. In the final analysis, despite their, in most cases, noble attempts to genuinely aid the black masses in this struggle, their existence was maintained directly at the expense of the masses. By placing their interests above those of the black masses, the black elite laid themselves open to future co-optation by the industrial financiers and politicians of white America. It was only a matter of time, therefore, before the partnership that is so characteristic of the situation existing today developed between them.

Even at this early date, it was recognized by a few in the black communities that the programs offered by the black elite were inadequate to meet the needs of the black masses. Interestingly, some of the spokesmen for the black elite at times themselves opposed some of the negative tendencies that put the making of money ahead of the liberation of black people. Though some of these men did not fully comprehend the nature of the American economic order, they sensed a certain futility in black people trying to imitate the masters of the capitalist system. Some even went so far as to suggest that black leaders should prepare black people to wage an armed struggle for the abolition of slavery in the South and poverty in the North.

Henry Highland Garnet's "Call to Rebellion" speech, delivered in 1843, and David Walker's "Appeal" in 1829, brilliantly reflect this sentiment. Frances Ellen Watkins echoed a similar message, when she wrote in the *Anglo-African* in 1859: "We need men and women whose hearts are the homes of a high and lofty enthusiasm, and a noble devotion to the cause of emancipation, who are ready and willing to lay time, talent and money on the altar of universal freedom." Miss Watkins then issued an obvious rebuke to the black elite: "We have money among us, but how much of it is spent to bring deliverance to our captive brethren?" Miss Watkins asked a very good question. Unfortunately it still awaits an answer today.

Miss Watkins's words were not very well received in many circles. It is little wonder that she and the other black revolutionaries of the North, such as Garnet and Walker, who refused to compromise on the needs of the black people, are seldom mentioned in the history books. The penetrating questions that they asked were, like those being asked today, looked upon with suspicion by white America and the black elite, both of which saw clearly in such legitimate expressions of opinion a potential threat to their economic interests. The black elite of the North to a great extent resisted the efforts of Miss Watkins, but when all was said and done they too were treated by white America like "field niggers."

At this point it would probably be fair to say that the years immediately preceding the Civil War for the first time offered black people in the North what they perceived as hope for the future. Black people began to feel that they possessed some measure of real power to effect a change in their conditions. With the advent of the Civil War and "emancipation," the aspirations of black America soared to even greater heights. And those aspirations seemed to bear some fruit in black economic successes. It was estimated at this time that the total real and personal wealth of black America totaled $50 million.[15] But most of this "economic gain" was concentrated largely in the hands of the still relatively small black elite. And this black elite could not be considered wealthy (much less independent) even by the financial indices of the nineteenth century.

As previously pointed out, the strong deterrents to the growth and accumulation of any real wealth or power among black people had by this time become well entrenched within the American structure. The two major determinants in the success of any business are the accessibility of capital and the availability of credit. The black elite, which already had after the war a partial base of operation in the black communities of the North, found both extremely hard to obtain. As far as the black masses were concerned, the economic situation was impossible. Every door was closed to them.

Black businesses had never been able to avail themselves of the capital and credit necessary to maintain anything other than marginal enterprises. One of the main factors, along with capitalism and its offspring, white racism, that strengthened the legacy of this development, was the gradual growth during this period of a patterned misleadership. This slowly became embedded within a black elite that persisted in wasting the valuable time, energy, and meager resources of the black masses trying to compete with white America's burgeoning monopoly capitalism.

Unfortunately, the post–Civil War period saw an intensification in the magnitude of this pattern. The federal government also played a large role in contributing to it. In 1865 the Freedmen's Bank was established through an act of Congress, signed by President Lincoln. The bank was originally intended to instill in the newly "emancipated" slaves the cherished Northern virtues of discipline and thrift in the handling of their personal finances. This supposedly represented a major contribution to the economic rehabilitation of black America.

Under the assumption that the Freedmen's Bank was to be protected by the government, black people rushed to entrust their small savings to it. Seven years after the end of the Civil War, the Freedmen's Bank claimed 70,000 depositors throughout the United States. The government naturally was pleased at the apparent success of its venture.

The optimistic note on which the bank was launched soon changed drastically. Despite assorted pretenses, it became clear to those involved in the bank's management that it was on the verge of collapse. A combination of factors, including graft, corruption, over-speculation, and general mismanagement of the bank's funds by its white trustees and managers, all were contributing to the bank's imminent demise. The general economic crisis that the nation was experiencing in the aftermath of the Civil War also brought pressure to bear upon the bank's security.

The white trustees of the bank, in a move to arrest this trend, elected Frederick Douglass president. Both Douglass and the trustees admitted that he had no experience in banking. Such a move clearly signified an attempt, on the part of the trustees, to capitalize on the name and popularity of Frederick Douglass among black people. It was hoped that this would serve as inducement to black people to continue investing their savings in the bank. Douglass himself eventually disclosed the dismal financial picture which faced the bank, that "the bank had, through dishonest agents, sustained heavy losses in the South, that there was a discrepancy on the books of forty thousand dollars for which no account could be given, and that, instead of our assets being equal to our liabilities, we could not in all likelihood of the case pay seventy-two cents on the dollar."[16]

From this point on, the Freedmen's Bank was a dead enterprise, but it was kept alive in the minds of the many black people who had invested all their faith and money in its success. The bank was closed approximately three months after Douglass's appointment as president. At Douglass's insistence, all the bank's resources were placed in the hands of commissioners for liquidation. The bank owed its 61,131 depositors $3 million, of which 62 percent was paid in dividends spread over an eight-year period from 1875 to 1883.[17] The Freedmen's Bank had been in existence barely nine years, from 1865 to 1874, before it collapsed.

Although many black people, and especially the freedmen, suffered hardship with the close of the bank, the experience gathered from the venture was not entirely lost, particularly for the black elite. It signaled for them a new shift for their programs. For the first time they saw new opportunities in the field of banking and finance, capitalism's major artery. And the training and preparation the Freedmen's Bank had provided them with proved later on to be the turning point in the history of black capitalism.

By 1888, a few black businessmen had joined together and organized the Capital Savings in Washington, D.C. A similar effort was undertaken in Richmond, Virginia, where the Grand Fountain United Order of True Reformers (Savings Bank) was founded. Over the following six-year period, from 1899 to 1905, twenty-eight banks were organized by the black elite. In the beginning, nearly all of these were created to serve as depositories for black fraternal orders.

It must be remembered that black people were almost totally insulated in their social existence from white America during this period. To offset this white racism, black fraternal and benevolent societies were formed to provide the black communities with a means of entertainment, recreation, and social life. The small amounts of money that the fraternal orders collected from these activities were, in varying degrees, initially used to finance banks.

By this time, the black elite had become thoroughly immersed in the idea of utilizing their banks to control the vital resources of black America. So-called black self-help programs were being devised by the black elite in the hopes of gaining the proper financial response to their enterprises from the black masses. The main problem that faced these aspiring black financiers was their inability to involve the total black community in any kind of sound long-range planning, planning based on principles of maximum distribution of benefits which, limited as those would be, would still represent an initial step in the right direction.

When one examines the record of their banks during the period of their greatest productivity—1888 to 1934—one finds there an answer to our central question: What became of the black elite's attempts to approach economic equality with white America? In this period, 134 banks were opened by the black elite throughout the black communities of both the North and the South. For the most part these were privately owned (often individually) and decidedly profit-oriented. The Forsyth Savings and Trust of Winston-Salem, North Carolina, was in operation twenty-two years (1907-1929). This marked the longest period of existence for any of the black elite's banks! Their peak year was 1926, when total resources for the estimated 35 banks then in existence was $13 million.

The stock crash of 1929 and the onset of world economic depression was a tremendous blow. By 1931 the total resources of these banks had decreased to $7 million, not much more than half the pre-1929 figure. By 1934 there were only 12 banks in existence. Today the number of black-owned (this in itself is always subject to question) banks in operation is placed at 22.[18]

The failure of the black elite's banks should not be viewed as an incidental or isolated occurrence. As Abram Harris accurately put it: "Given sound and honest management, the Negro bank would still face one fundamental and perhaps insuperable obstacle to successful operation, namely, the inherent characteristics of Negro business enterprise." [19] There is a direct correlation between the collapse of the banks and the failure of black business in general. The area of banking illustrates the point quite well, but this also could apply to any of the other fields in which the black elite had chosen to invest.

Some of the other types of business enterprise in which the black elite were engaged included tailoring and clothing, a few newspapers, cooking and livery stables. Insurance business also figured prominently in the financial activities of the black elite. And, just as in banking, the black insurance companies' contribution to the economic development of the black communities was negligible. As an example, it was calculated that during this period a single large white insurance company carried policies on more black lives than twice the volume carried by all black insurance companies put together![*1]

The Depression of the 1930s wiped out much of the black elite's precariously built economic base within black America. Black businesses, many already operating on either the marginal incomes of their proprietors from other jobs or the individual's life savings, were forever lost. This should have been enough to awaken the black elite to the fact that white monopoly capitalism is the all-controlling factor in the economic life of America. If it suffers a setback (the Depression is the best example), the first to feel the reverberations has always been the weakest interest group in American society—namely the black elite.

To understand thoroughly the historic development of this process under American capitalism and its implications for the future, a further examination of black business in the immediate post–Civil War era is necessary. The first survey of black businesses was conducted in 1898. It was found that the average capital investment of the 1,906 black businesses replying to the survey's questionnaire amounted to only $4,600.[20] This figure was considered an impressive accomplishment by the black elites, and the effect was to give added impetus to the illusion shared by many black businessmen that the black community could in fact sustain an independent, self-sufficient economy. As Abram Harris has stated: "The Negro masses, urged by their leaders, were led to place increasing faith in business and property as a means of escaping poverty and achieving economic independence. . . . Negro business enterprise was motivated primarily by

---

* This pattern remains unchanged today. North Carolina Mutual Life Insurance Co. is the largest black insurance operation in the country today. Its assets total $94 million. By comparison, Prudential, one of white America's largest insurance companies, has assets of $25 billion! Altogether the top five black insurance companies' combined assets, roughly $268 million, equal little more than 1 percent of Prudential's assets alone.

the desire for private profit and looked toward the establishment of a Negro capitalist employer class." [21]

Professor Harris cites the proceedings of the Fourth Atlanta University Conference on the Negro in Business which was held in 1898. The first resolution adopted by the conference is perhaps best illustrative of the mood and direction of its participants. The first part of this resolution was essentially an exercise in the use of rhetoric. The call was for greater support and participation of the black masses in business; this was to be the means for the economic vitalization of black America, in the same mode as white America. The resolution concludes, and here the real intent becomes clear, by rekindling the spirit of Delaney's message of a half-century earlier. It notes the rise of U.S. capitalism as an international force. The black elite then proposes, through an illogic generated by unreasoned analysis, that the black masses could do the same by encouraging "the growth of a class of merchants." [22]

The conference mainly succeeded in renewing the pledge of a century past to create a black business establishment capable of imitating in the black community the successes of American capitalism in the world. This came at a time when the American government had embarked on a policy of world imperialist expansion. The United States, through military force, had established footholds in Cuba, Latin America, the Pacific islands, and some parts of Asia. The black elite viewed this naked military-economic aggression as a healthy sign of white America's strength and vitality. As today, they were engaged in a desperate search for some method of operation that would first ensure them a share in the wealth, and second, if possible, bridge the economic gap which separated the black masses from other workers. Capitalism seemed the logical means. The only problem with this was that white America's imperialist expansion depended on both foreign and *domestic* colonial subjugation, and the prime victim of the latter was black America, collectively.

Thus the black elite ushered in the twentieth century with an optimistic exuberance based more on their personal dreams of financial empire than on an understanding or acknowledgment of the expectations of the black masses.

In several cities at this time, certain trade and service enterprises were almost exclusively dominated by the black elite. In Charleston, South Carolina, it was the butcher and barber shops; in Philadelphia, black businessmen predominated in the catering services; and in Atlanta the black elite had acquired large interests in contracting and real estate.

In 1900, Booker T. Washington organized the National Negro Business League (NNBL). The League was dedicated to building the influence of businesses and organizing other business leagues in every black community in the country. Washington, as the League's spokesman, repeatedly urged black people to explore the new "opportunities" opening up in the field of business. He couched his enthusiasm for the League's accomplishments in terms designed to appeal to all segments of black America. As he put it, "The National Negro Business League ... has brought to view from far and wide many business enterprises which were not known beyond the immediate town or vicinity in which they are located." [23]

The message that Washington and his NNBL carried was warmly received by the black elite. They were quite pleased to enlist the services of such a nationally prominent figure as Booker T. Washington to lend credence to their campaign for black business expansion. By 1907, the NNBL could claim that 300 additional business leagues had been formed in various locales throughout the country. Washington, until his death in 1915, was named to successive terms as president of the NNBL. Moved by the apparent acceptance by the black masses of his pronouncements on black business expansion, Washington in 1907 published a book called *The Negro in Business*. In it he pointedly detailed individual cases of black people who had achieved "success" in the ownership and operation of a variety of business enterprises.[24]

With the future seemingly secured for black people in business, the NNBL established a subsidiary organization, the Colored Merchants Association. The CMA sought to set up a chain of grocery stores in black communities across the country. The end result of this plan proved quite disappointing to the CMA. Its eventual failure was assured largely because of two factors: the traditional lack of business experience of the prospective black merchants, and lack of support from the black communities.

The NNBL itself has witnessed a steady growth over the years. Today it lists more than 10,000 members on its roster. But although various structural changes have taken place within the organization, a proportional increase in the number of black businesses has not been forthcoming. Many listed members are not really engaged in the operation of any business. The organization has dropped the word "Negro" from its title; now it is simply the National Business League. Apparently this move was made to attract support for its programs from people outside the black community.

Though the NNBL, from the beginning, was organized and managed by Booker T. Washington, it was financed for the most part by Washington's white industrialist benefactors, led by Andrew Carnegie. This in itself pointed up the black elite's dilemma. By 1900, after nearly one hundred years of extolling the benefits of black business solvency, the black elite was not even in a position to finance its own organization. Even more damaging to the black elite's case for the benefits of business was the fact that leading white capitalist financiers such as Carnegie could feel it expedient to finance a black organization. This simply testified to the extensive role which corporate capitalism was beginning to play in the black communities. As a tactical move, it was necessary even then to promote the weak interests of the black elite. By doing this, capitalism would build into the social framework of the black community a strategically manipulable, divisive element. All this was done under the guise of "philanthropic aid."

The noted historian Benjamin Quarles has perhaps best

summed up the tragedy of misdirection that characterized the
NNBL at its inception:

> The League emphasis rested on the accepted values of the nine-
> teenth century . . . at a time when reformers were beginning to
> plead for government aid in controlling aggressive monopoly,
> finance capitalism, exploitation of labor, and slums. In holding
> up the small businessman as a prototype, Washington and the
> League obscured from race vision some other legal means by
> which white businessmen forged ahead.[25]

Washington, as a historical figure, deserves special attention.
Perhaps more than any other black leader, he advanced the notion
of a separate black economy. In the famed speech delivered at
the Atlanta Exposition in 1895, he set the tone for that decade
when he said: "Ignorant and inexperienced, it is not strange that
in the first years of our new life we began at the top instead of the
bottom; that a seat in Congress or the State Legislature was more
sought than real estate or industrial skill; that the political convention or stump speaking had more attractions than starting a dairy
farm or truck garden." Washington was immediately catapulted
into national prominence as a result of this speech. The financial
coffers of corporate America slowly began to open to him.

As with black capitalism today, Washington's non-threatening
brand of black economic development found a ready appeal
with the captains of American finance capitalism. His great
influence with white financiers such as John D. Rockefeller,
Julius Rosenwald, Andrew Mellon, H. H. Rogers, and Andrew
Carnegie, to name a few, enabled him to expand greatly the programs he had designed to push his accommodationist line of
economic withdrawal as a substitute for, rather than as a supple-
ment to, independent black political struggle. Through control
of various black newspapers around the country, Washington
was able to sway black public opinion toward emulation and
acceptance of the most negative values in American society. As an

indication of Washington's power, he was able to induce Julius Rosenwald to invest $30,000 in the all-black town of Mound Bayou, Mississippi's cotton-oil mill.

Mound Bayou was originally founded by Isaiah T. Montgomery, a former slave of Jefferson Davis, in 1887. In time Montgomery became a close personal friend of Washington's, and one of the main exponents of his program in the South. Montgomery gained further notoriety when he openly defended the Mississippi Constitutional Convention's disfranchisement of blacks in 1890. With this action, Montgomery dramatically exemplified the complete contempt in which Washington supporters held any effort by blacks to gain political power.

Further, at one point public criticism of his policies had reached such a level of intensity that in 1904 Washington found it expedient to call a secret meeting of black leaders from around the country. The meeting was financed by Andrew Carnegie and held in Carnegie Hall in New York. The Carnegie Hall Conference, as it came to be called, established a Committee of Twelve for the Advancement of the Interests of the Negro Race. The Committee published a series of pamphlets, all financed by Carnegie, which dealt with various aspects of black business development. A few of the pamphlets were reprints of speeches by some of the country's most outspokenly reactionary white businessmen. Of course, all of the material published was carefully selected by Washington.

Until 1911, Carnegie contributed $2,700 yearly to the financing of the NNBL's annual convention. The two following quotations from Andrew Carnegie and William Dean Howells, respectively, provide a good estimate of just how prominently Washington's ideas figured in the plans of the white corporate businessmen of that day.

CARNEGIE: "Booker Washington's influence is powerfully exerted to keep the negroes from placing suffrage in the front. He contends that good moral character and industrial efficiency, resulting in the ownership of property, are the pressing needs and the sure and speedy path to recognition and enfranchisement. A few able negroes are disposed to press for the free and unrestricted vote immediately. We cannot but hope that the wiser policy will prevail." (From a speech delivered before the Philosophical Institute of Edinburgh, 1907.)

HOWELLS: "Booker T. Washington has made himself a public man, second to no other American in importance. He seems to hold in his grasp the key to the situation; for if his notion of reconciling the Anglo-American to the Afro-American, by a civilization which shall not threaten the Anglo-American supremacy, is not the key what is? He imagines for his race a civilization industrial and economical, hoping for the virtues which spring from endeavor and responsibility; and apparently his imagination goes no further." ("An Exemplary Citizen," *North American Review* 173, August 1901: 281–88.)

In 1928, the NNBL undertook a partial survey of black businesses in the United States. A total of 1,534 business enterprises in 33 cities was included in the survey. It was found that the overwhelming bulk of the enterprises did an annual gross business of less than $5,000; less than 10 percent of these enterprises even approached $10,000 in their annual gross. The survey further revealed that on the average only 3.9 persons were employed in each business establishment. The sample survey figures represent, on the whole, sorry testimony to NNBL's accomplishments during its first quarter-century of existence. Except for a few banks and a small scattering of insurance companies, the black elite had no control over any real industrial or commercial enterprises functioning either in or outside of the black communities.*[2]

---

* Actually, during this period a slow but steady decline was beginning in the development of black business. In 1898, the average volume of business done by the 1,906 black businesses surveyed was $4,600. In 1944, the figure for some 3,866 black businesses in 12 cities stood at only $3,260. See Joseph A. Pierce, *Negro Business and Business Education* (New York: Harper, 1947), 69.

The early 1920s, it can be said, were characterized by intensive efforts to develop black businesses into a competitive force capable of standing up against white capitalism. The black elite, during the 1920s, held the institutions of corporate capitalism in such awe that they began to adopt their names. For instance, in 1921 a group of black businessmen in New York founded the Harlem Stock Exchange. A similar venture was undertaken in Detroit in 1926. As one might expect, both were short-lived.

Surprising as it may seem, a chief standard bearer of what can be labeled the "black business syndrome" was none other than the illustrious Marcus Garvey. Garvey came to the United States in 1919 to meet with Booker T. Washington. He clearly felt that the economic philosophy that guided his own thought closely paralleled Washington's. Garvey therefore concluded that the movement he had begun in Jamaica in 1914, the Universal Negro Improvement Association, could unite and work with Washington's organization.

Many blacks today are beginning to recognize the similarities, not only between the ideas of Washington and Garvey, but also among those held by other black nationalist figures. Harold Cruse, in his work *Rebellion or Revolution?* has accurately pointed out: "The present slogan of Black Power is nothing more than a shifting back to the basic position taken by Booker T. Washington in 1900 with the addition, of course, of certain contemporary refinements. When the CORE and SNCC 'direct action' protest-civil righters make a turnabout and say:

- Give up 'integration' efforts . . .
- De-emphasize civil rights protests . . .
- Stop agitation for more worthless civil rights bills . . .
- Let us go back into the black communities and build our own economic, educational, and political institution . . .
- Let us build 'Black Power'! then we'll be 'equal'!

What real difference is there between these slogans of today and those of Booker T. Washington in 1900 when he said:

- Brains, money, property, education . . .
- Plenty of good schools and good teachers . . .
- Tone down worthless civil rights protests . . .
- Let us build our group economic power . . .
- Let us have good farms, good businesses, thriving cooperatives . . .
- Let us establish these things for ourselves and all civil rights will be added as a matter of course, for we will then be truly equal.

Cruse, whether through oversight or conscious effort, neglects to add here the marked similarity between Carnegie's and Rosenwald's support of Washington in 1900 and the Ford Foundation and Rockefeller support of black nationalists such as Roy Innis today. Cruse, despite the perceptiveness of his analogy, completely misrepresents Washington's purpose. As already shown, Washington's program was not, as Cruse intimates, progressive. It was explicitly designed to promote the fortunes of a tiny black merchant and propertied class rather than the collective economic development of the black masses.

Although Garvey's plans were cut short by Washington's death, he always felt an admiring kinship to him, and thereafter referred to Washington as the "sage of Tuskegee." Garvey's early interest in and acceptance of Washington's program was to color much of his future action in the United States: "I read *Up from Slavery*, by Booker T. Washington, and then my doom—if I may so call it—of being a race leader dawned upon me."[26]

In order to carry out his program, Garvey skillfully employed various slogans and concepts of black cultural thought to appeal directly to the nationalism latent in the spirit of the black masses.

This proved quite successful in gaining him the acceptance and support of the black masses. As part of his economic program, he set up the Black Star Steamship Line and the Negro Factories Corporation. The Black Star Line was part of an intricate plan to purchase, through the sale of stock, a chain of ships to carry black people back to Africa. The Negro Factories Corporation was established with the intention of developing black business opportunities within the United States. The Factories Corporation was eventually able to develop such businesses as a restaurant, a chain of cooperative grocery stores, a steam laundry, a tailoring and dressmaking shop, a millinery store, and a publishing house.[27] Although the Black Star Line was intended as an exclusively black operation, it is interesting to note that at least five key positions were filled by white men.

While busy promoting black business interests, Garvey was at all times adamant in his opposition to communism. He fell right in line behind America's white corporate rulers. He proclaimed that the "only convenient friend" that the black masses should consider was none other than the "white capitalist."[28] In several astounding pronouncements, Garvey practically thanked America's industrialists for employing black workers, even while conceding that it was on the most menial level with the lowest possible wages. Harold Cruse, writing from the posture of black cultural nationalism, capsulized the emphasis of the Garvey program : "By the time Garvey arrived with his program, the entire colonial world was passing from anti-imperialism to anti-capitalism as a way of economic organization. Yet Garvey's program remained pro-capitalist during its 1920s era."[29] Cruse notes further that even today the few remaining disciples who keep alive the nostalgia of Garvey's movement still hold to the fundamental belief that black capitalism is a potential force for the political-economic reconstruction of the African continent.

Still, Garvey's impact on black America was enormous. At the height of his career, he had moved to a position of power unequaled to this day by any black nationalist leader in America.

Garvey's UNIA could claim a membership of nearly a million black people, with an even larger number of sympathizers and admirers spread throughout the country.

Through cultural nationalism, Garvey was able to sell his ideas on black capitalism to the black masses better than any of the traditional spokesmen for the black elite had ever been able to do. Thousands of black people across the country invested enormous sums of money in his organization's business ventures. The Black Star Line alone, in one year and through the sale of various stocks and subscriptions to black people, achieved a capital of $610,860.[30] All too often, the money that was invested represented the hard-earned life savings of many in black America. According to some estimates, a million dollars at the very least was lost by black investors. Approximately $800,000 was tied up in the Black Star Line alone, and the Line consisted of four broken-down, outdated ships. The story told by the above figures is that black people, through unqualified faith and desperate hope, gave to the Garvey program as they had never given before.

Unfortunately, as should have been expected, most of this money was lost when Garvey's enterprises and plans fell through. The dreams of liberation of millions of black people in America (and the world, for Garvey's movement was truly international in scope and numbers) died when Garvey was jailed, allegedly for fraud, and later deported. The experience of Marcus Garvey, heir apparent to the dead Booker T. Washington's program of economic nationalism, provided a lesson which the black masses and the black elite have still largely not absorbed.

That lesson is that no matter how large or well organized a black political or social movement becomes, those involved must be equipped with the proper understanding of the American economic order. Unless they are, they will never use the correct approach in determining methods for the struggle against the conditions of corporate capitalism that are impoverishing black America.

The pattern set by Garvey was carried over into the Depression years of the 1930s. The black elite was by now feverish in its attempts to retain the marginal economic foothold it had in black communities. St. Clair Drake and Horace Cayton, in their work *Black Metropolis,* point out that one of the main factors in this upsurge of activity was the mass migration to the Northern cities of black people from the rural South following World War I. This of course increased substantially both the number and size of the North's black ghettos, and as a natural result greatly expanded the black consumer market.

The black elite sought to exploit this to the fullest. Numerous "Buy Black" drives were launched. Almost overnight many new black businesses were opened to capture a share in the new bustling black consumer market. Soon, Buy Black became such an appealing slogan that the black elite united it with a new economic program which they had devised.

It was labeled the "Double-Duty Dollar Plan." The black elite contended that if black people patronized black businesses they would help to bolster the economic strength of "their" businesses while at the same time creating jobs for black people within their community. It was also noted that the Buy Black—Double-Duty Dollar program was pushed to a great extent by black ministers (many of whom coincidentally owned business enterprises of their own). Acting in collusion with the black elite, the black minister-businessman accused any black person who questioned the validity of the black elite's program of being a hindrance to black unity.

The trend in the black church toward business investment is directly traceable to the early influence of Washington. Black ministers were always much in evidence at the annual meeting of the NNBL. At the sixteenth annual session of the NNBL, for example, a well-known Nashville preacher-businessman, the Reverend R. H. Boyd, asserted in a speech that discrimination provided a means of building economic independence among blacks: "These discriminations are only blessings in disguise.

They stimulate and encourage rather than cower and humiliate the true, ambitious, self-determined Negro."

The figures related by Drake and Cayton in *Black Metropolis*, their book on life in Chicago's black ghetto, show that by 1938 there were a total of 2,600 black businesses in Chicago. The major types of businesses operated are shown in the following partial breakdown: 287 beauty parlors; 257 grocery stores; 207 barber shops; 163 tailors, cleaners, and pressers; and 145 restaurants. At the same time, there were some 2,800 white business enterprises in Chicago's black community.[31] Further, it was noted that although black business enterprises comprised nearly one-half of all businesses in the black community, less than one-tenth of the money spent by the black consumer went to black businesses.

A previous business census taken in 1935 also supported this finding. This survey revealed that of the $11 million spent on groceries in the black community, only 5 percent was spent in black-owned grocery stores. The unwillingness of black people to support black businesses has been fairly common throughout the country. Frazier has documented this phenomenon on the national level: "Although Negro businesses are operated primarily for Negroes, the total volume of sales of [black-owned] food stores, according to the United States Census of Business in 1939, was only $24,037,000, or less than two dollars for each Negro in the United States."[32]

Why was there such a large disparity between the number of black businesses and the small total volume of business done by them? At least part of the answer is provided when one examines the patterns that emerged in the operation of the black businesses. An independent business survey was conducted at this time. It found that all black-owned businesses were located in either exclusively all-black communities or mixed neighborhoods which, it is safe to say, were changing into black ghettos. The survey also indicated that fully 85 percent of all black businesses were one-man establishments, while another 9 percent were partnerships; 3 percent were corporations; and only 1 percent cooperatives.[33]

The figures presented here are descriptive of both the level and the overall direction of operation to which the black business enterprises were geared. The vast majority of these businesses were unable to give employment to anyone in the black communities other than the owner himself. And, most important of all, the black elite almost unanimously attempted to operate their businesses within the guidelines laid down by American capitalism. In this light, it was truly amazing that even 1 percent of these black businesses considered an alternative mode of operation, which the cooperative enterprise represented.

Some further figures from this survey, which covered 12 cities, provide even more illuminating indicators by which to evaluate the performance of black business. Atlanta, Georgia, had the largest number of black businesses, 845. Washington, D.C., with 696 black businesses, stood second. In Washington, nearly 90 percent of black businesses were single proprietorships. The median volume of business done by each of these enterprises was $4,500. The average employee count for each establishment was 3.8. The weekly salary for each employee averaged out to $31.[34]

The largest field of concentration for these black businesses was within the traditional pattern: namely, the service establishments—barber shops, beauty parlors, restaurants, cleaners, etc. It should be remembered that service enterprises have, throughout the history of black capitalism in America, been the only area of enterprise in this country in which the black elite could lay any claim to acceptance. After all, a barber shop or beauty parlor can easily be opened, in some cases with the most minimal amount of capital. Since most of the black businesses that have failed have been in the service areas, it is by now clear that they can fold just as easily as they can be opened.

As a matter of record, the only kind of black business in the service area that has enjoyed any semblance of lasting success over the years has been the funeral parlor. This has been due to the segregated existence forced upon the black communities, since it has been traditional that white undertakers refuse to make funeral arrangements for black people in white cemeteries. The economic benefit to black undertakers, then, has grown only out of absolute necessity, and has never represented any special area of economic breakthrough by the black elite.

In further reviewing black capitalism in the early decades of the twentieth century, a sad note must be added. This is the story of Madame C. J. Walker and the growth of the cosmetics industry. Madame Walker was one of the first black millionaires in the United States.[*3] She made her fortune through the manufacture and sale of hair and skin preparations in black communities. Madame Walker admitted that while walking down the street one day it suddenly occurred to her that black people wanted very much to look like white people. She therefore proceeded to devise a vast array of skin creams and whiteners, hair pomades and various concocted chemicals, for straightening and processing hair.

The black elite wasted little time in exploiting these products to the fullest. It was quite evident to them that the pitiable escapist dreams of the black masses could be materially productive. By 1938 there were more than a dozen companies set up for the sole purpose of manufacturing hair and skin preparations. These companies together represented more than one-third of all the manufacturing enterprises owned by the black elite,[35] and their products were so popular that their sale kept many barber shops and beauty parlors in the black communities from financial collapse. In fact, many new outlets were opened to market the products and ensure their widest possible dispersal throughout the black communities.

I have called this kind of business "sad." What other term

---

* Between the end of the Civil War and 1912, R. R. Church, a black businessman in Memphis, reportedly built up a million-dollar fortune in real estate speculation and investment.

could depict accurately the spectacle in which beautiful Africoid features of natural bushy hair and smooth dark skin were, through the use of chemicals, turned into grotesque caricatures? This was the culminating attempt to obliterate all remnants of an honorable and great African past shared by all black people in the United States. Even more tragic was the widespread feeling among black people, that they could somehow transcend their color, and thereby their oppressive conditions, and become— white. It was supposed that this would mean acceptance. In short, black people were made to feel both a psychological and physical hate for their very persons. With this, white racist oppression had finally completed its task of making black people (the slaves) ashamed and scornful of themselves for being in their situation (slavery) instead of angry at the real cause, the dominance of corporate capitalism. That the black elite would sacrifice the little self-respect left the black masses for a comparatively few dollars reflected very unadmirably on its character.

The history of black capitalism would not be complete without a look at another of its aspects, one overlooked or summarily dismissed in most analyses of black business. That is the role of the "policy," which particularly in the 1930s had considerable control of the economic life in the black communities of the North.

The "policy," or what is commonly referred to as the "numbers game," played a significant part in the financing of many enterprises in the black communities during the 1920s and 1930s. In Chicago alone, it was estimated that nearly one-quarter of the largest black businesses were either owned or controlled by the policy syndicate. At a black business exposition held in Chicago in 1938, 14 of the 87 businesses represented were owned by policy interests.[36] And it was in the policy that the greatest opportunities existed for an individual black person to make a fortune literally overnight.

Nearly every segment of the black community, from ministers through the politicians and police, had some interest in the policy. The policy syndicate, like other black businesses, was visibly controlled by the black elite. However, in the policy, unlike many other black businesses, the black elite was often simply acting on behalf of the outside white interests who really controlled it.

It came as little surprise to find many of the so-called respectable members of the black elite praising the policy. It was seen by many in the black elite as being a financial boost to the "economy" of the black community. It was argued that the policy created new jobs and income for black people. The cultism that surrounds capitalism as a cure-all for economic problems—"if only I can get some of it"—was given added credence by the relation of the policy to the black community. On this Drake and Cayton have written: "The policy kings have been enthusiastic proponents of the myth of 'racial salvation by Negro business.' They have given some reality to the hope of erecting an independent economy within Black Metropolis (Chicago's black ghetto)."[37] Instead of reality, the correct term here would be "illusion." The real reality of the situation was that the policy syndicate, like a few other black business enterprises, reaped large profits from the labor and enslaved condition of the black masses. For example, the owners of three policy companies grossed over $10,000 in net income for one week (and this was in 1938!).[38] Compare this to the median return for "legitimate" black businesses, which was around $4,000 a year, and one can readily see that the policy was indeed a lucrative undertaking. In fact, outside of the black church, the policy syndicate was undoubtedly the best organized and most extensive business operation in the black communities. As Frazier has pointed out: "At the summer resorts where the black bourgeoisie gather to display their wealth, descendants of the old respectable families must defer to the underworld elements, who, through their money, have risen to the top of Negro 'society.'"

Needless to say, the main interest of policy operators was not to establish something of real benefit to blacks, such as educational funds or consumer education courses, but to maximize their profits. After all, the policy, legal or illegal, was still a capitalistic business operation. The promoters of the policy quite naturally got richer and richer. In some cases they felt it necessary to put up a facade of respectability. This could only be done by creating situations in which it appeared that the policy operators were truly interested in helping people in the black communities. The establishment of legitimate business enterprises by the policy operators was the handiest method of doing this. These businesses, some of which also served as operational fronts, could be pointed to by the black elite as being examples of black self-help. But the fact of the matter was, the policy syndicate never made any long-term developmental investment in the disjointed socioeconomic structure of any black community, including Harlem. Despite all the propagandists' claims the black elite made about the supposed improvements and contributions the policy made, the economic conditions of the Northern black ghetto continued to deteriorate. Only with the coming of World War II did the plight of the black masses begin to change. Then, American industry was for the first time forced, because of the severe manpower shortage, to open up new jobs for black people in the factories and plants on a large scale.

Not to mention a threat made by A. Philip Randolph to march on Washington, D.C., with 100,000 unemployed black workers if discrimination in employment was not eliminated. This, as is known, prompted President Roosevelt to sign an executive order banning racial discrimination in defense plants and establishing a Fair Employment Practices Committee to enforce the directive.

Clearly, during its early period of existence black capitalism in any form did not make a dent in the all-embracing destitution suffered by the black masses. On the contrary, like its protector, American corporate capitalism, it polarized the black community to the point where a small clique tightened its hold on the reins of leadership. The black masses remained on the bottom rung of the economic ladder and controlled nothing. And, ironically, never during this period was the black elite able to claim any real personal wealth or power, much less any wealth or power that could be used to supply even the most minimal of black America's needs.

It can justifiably be said, then, that all the attempts that were made during this period to shape white America's capitalist structure into a black elite–dominated system for developing the productive potential of black America failed. A legacy of misleadership evolved from this failure, and has been the predominant factor in the past and present programmatic planning of black America's spokesmen and thinkers. This is true despite the shift in emphasis from Booker T. Washington's economic nationalism to Martin Luther King's program of integration.

And now, among some, the cycle has been set in motion again, with King's concept of integration giving way to a revival of Garvey's mixed program of cultural-economic nationalism. It would perhaps be wise to examine next some aspects of the role religion has played in the development of black economic determinism.

2

Black Religion and Capitalism

In the social conditions surrounding the lives of black people on the white plantation during slavery, many white slave masters considered the church and religion a prime psychological asset. Under the strict control of a clever master, the church served as a natural safety valve, through which much of the resentment and hostility felt by black people toward their condition could be channeled into an acceptable and harmless escapism.

As LeRoi Jones (later Amiri Baraka) has noted:

> The slave masters also learned early that the Africans who had begun to accept the Christian ethic or even some crude part of. its dogma were less likely to run away or start rebellions or uprisings. Christianity ... was to be used strictly as a code of conduct which would enable its devotees to participate in an after life; it was from its very inception among the black slaves, a slave ethic.

In time, the church became the only institution genuinely worthy of the name to develop among black people. On the plantation, it became the major center of social activity.

For the most part, the appeal of the church stemmed from the indescribable physical misery of slavery; but another factor that influenced its rise was the traditional emphasis African society had placed on spiritual values. The residual effects of this emphasis on the spiritual were carried over and retained as a feature of the collective character of black people in America. This tended to give the church even more of an emotive appeal to black people. LeRoi Jones, in describing the deep emotional or "soul" feeling especially akin to black people, has appropriately used the term "blues people," in symbolic reference. These two aspects of the black heritage, African spiritualism and American slavery, combined to create a deep social and psychological desire within the black masses for a strong independent force that could deliver them from the oppressive conditions forced upon them.

The growth in the late eighteenth century of the free black population in many Northern cities ushered in a new phase in the development of the black church. In Philadelphia in 1786, Richard Allen founded the African Methodist Episcopal Church (AME). (This, by the way, was the Richard Allen most instrumental in organizing the first "mutual aid" society, referred to previously.) With the founding of the AME church, Allen moved religion among black people to a new level of organization. This marked the beginning of the black elite's interest in religion as a source of profit. The organized church could provide an individual or a group with the means for retaining long-term control over the financial resources of the black masses: a ready-made opportunity for the economic exploitation of the black community. As a result, the black church, after passing through the phase of formal organization, came to the point where its very existence was based on conflicting purposes. It served a function in providing comfort and temporary refuge for black people. But at the same time, the black church's leadership became increasingly preoccupied with the idea of securing for themselves an interest in the "fortunes" of black business. Black ministers, in all too many cases, soon began to abdicate their supposed first

concern—the black community's well-being—and run the affairs
of the church on a strictly financial basis. The church became
simply another business, where success was measured not by
the number of needy black people helped, but by the number
of dollars "earned." In many black churches, the minister lived
for the Sunday collections and always kept a watchful lookout
for the chance to increase the size of the donations he received.
Obviously then, it was no accident that the black minister grew to
be, as a matter of tradition, one of the wealthiest and hence most
respected members of the black community. The black minister,
through the church, became so successful that he inspired many
other opportunistic hustlers in the black community to go into
business for themselves. Soon, anyone who could get a few chairs
and a room was immediately liable to call himself "Reverend"
and try to pass himself off on the black community as a man with
a divine calling. This to a degree also explains the predominance
in black communities today of what is commonly called the
"storefront church."

The "Double-Duty Dollar" doctrine has become the order
of the day in the black church. Advertisements carried in the
newspapers of black churches advocate patronizing certain black
businesses. Drake and Cayton have noted that "specific businessmen are often pointed out to the congregations as being worthy
of emulation and support." By the 1930s, the black church had
become a main agent for promoting the interests of a few select
business enterprises belonging to the black elite. In actuality, the
working relationship that developed was a de facto agreement
between the two non-competing factions of the black elite that
the black minister and black businessman represented. The
intent was to increase the power, prestige, and financial resources
of the black elite within black America.

The Father Divine Peace Movement was perhaps the best
example of this. This group, concentrated mainly in the Harlem
of the 1930s, was the first really mass-based black spiritual movement in the United States. The movement's newspaper, *New*

Day, carried regular advertisements of various national and local business firms. The followers of Father Divine were strongly urged to establish their own businesses in conjunction with the movement. Father Divine himself achieved millionaire status and was ranked by *Ebony* magazine in 1949 as one of the ten richest black persons in the United States.[1] As Drake and Cayton summed it up:

> This endorsement of business by the church simply dramatizes, and brings the force of sacred sanctions to bear upon, slogans that the press, the civic organizations, and even the social clubs repeat incessantly, emphasizing the duty of Negroes to trade with Negroes and promising ultimate racial "salvation" if they will support racial business enterprises.[2]

Categorically stated, the black church, from the lofty position it has consistently occupied in both the spiritual consciousness and the physical life of the black masses, has been able to control more of the black community's minuscule financial resources than any other type of single or collective black business enterprise. By condition of its existence as a segregated institution in America, the black church has always contained a seed of religious separatism which has at times produced a ritualistic mysticism. In the early part of the twentieth century, this seed flowered in several black nationalistic religious sects with dedicated followings. The most successful were the Daddy Grace and the Prophet Jones movements. Of lesser note, but important as a forerunner of the modern-day Nation of Islam's economic-religious nationalism, was the Moorish movement of Noble Drew Ali.

Noble Drew Ali founded the Moorish-American Science Temple in Newark in 1913. The Moorish movement owed its spiritual allegiance to Islam. Drew Ali considered it his divine mission to convert all black people in the United States to the Islamic religion. As leader of the Moorish movement, he set up numerous small businesses within various black communities, all under the ownership of the members of his movement. With this development, black religious nationalism had firmly staked its future on the viability of black business.

But Drew Ali's Moorish movement broke up when he was jailed in 1929 for the alleged murder of a rival member of his organization, just as UNIA dissolved when Garvey was jailed for fraud. Out of this movement's factional split grew the Nation of Islam, under the direction of the mysterious W. D. Fard. The leadership soon thereafter passed into the hands of the Honorable Elijah Muhammad.

After Garvey and Drew Ali's departure from the scene, the Nation continued, along with the black elite, to attempt to implement a program of black business development. Unlike the black elite, the Nation has skillfully combined the nationalist features of the Garvey movement and the religious-separatist character of the Noble Drew Ali movement to achieve this end. The Nation of Islam first gained national prominence in the late 1950s, largely as a result of the reports of the white news media. Since then, the Nation has provided black communities with a most highly organized, conscientious image of black business in actual development.

From its very inception the philosophy of the Nation has found a practical expression in the area of black business enterprise. The Nation's religious orientation is strongly rooted in the precedents established by the earlier black religious-separatist movements, which include foremost an emphasis on black economic "self-help." Therefore, the key to understanding the Nation's traditional emphasis on black business lies directly in the prominent role Christianity has played in shaping much of black America's thoughts and actions. The Nation's hierarchy has never been under the exclusive control of the black elite. However, in practice their political stance—non-participation—and their tactical approach, building up a black business structure, often effect the same result as the black elite.

To some extent, the overt black nationalist appeals made by the

Nation to the black community have irritated other segments of the black elite, the black professional in particular. This element has been prompted at various times to join with white "liberals" in attacking the Nation, usually with such absurd accusations as that the Nation is an "extremist" force which teaches hate and violence toward the white man. And, as is apparent by now, the black elite's criticism is prompted by fear and to a certain extent jealousy. The black elite, as opposed to the Nation, has always preferred the approach of ever-so-subtly appealing to the feeling of black unity, while reaping financial profits in the black communities.

The Nation, like the UNIA earlier, has, by comparison, gained greater access to the economy of the black community than has the black elite. This success has led it to revive the old idea of creating an independent black economic base capable of providing for the needs of the black community. Mr. Muhammad has set forth a five-point program which he envisions as the basis for future black economic planning. This program has been titled "Economic Blue Print for the Black Man." The first four points stress the need for unity in the building of a black economy. In itself, this represents sound programmatic reasoning and would logically serve as a positive step in raising the black community's level of consciousness. Revolutionary awareness can only be attained through a series of struggles, each building upon the other in successive stages, the end result being black solidarity in political or social action. The fifth point in Mr. Muhammad's program, however, leaves little doubt as to where he stands in his approach to the problem of black economic development: "Observe the operations of the White Man. He is successful. He makes no excuses for his failure. He works hard—in a collective manner. You do the same." [3]

In formulating this last point in his economic program, Mr. Muhammad reveals the deep-rooted imitative tendency inherent in the thought of the black leadership, nearly all of whom strongly identify in one way or another with the capitalist power of white America. Nationalists included, they feel, as Mr. Muhammad's economic program graphically demonstrates, that greater shares in the American corporate economy will solve the crises of black America. Mr. Muhammad's willingness to incorporate into his program the very qualities in the capitalist system directly responsible for the current economic strain upon the average worker (black and white) indicates that he feels strongly that part of white America's economic structure can be adapted to meet the needs of black people. Nonetheless, this has served to create the suspicion in some blacks that his program contains a very definable potential for co-optation. This has of course been characteristic of the programs of the black elite.

The Nation's unique interpretation of the principles of positive economic nationalism, the most important of which is unity through collective struggle, not imitation, has in some instances created strains within the black communities. Mr. Muhammad attributes the phenomenal rate of economic growth enjoyed by U.S. capitalism to a collective spirit supposedly possessed by white people in general. The fallaciousness of the thought on this point is apparent when one examines the socioeconomic patterns of white America. The spirit of American capitalism is far from collective. An extreme disparity does exist between the average white worker and the relatively few giant white corporate bodies. It is not simply a problem, as has been suggested, of white people collectively prospering, for most of the poverty in the United States is in white America, not black. According to government figures, nearly twenty million white people were below the poverty line in 1967 as opposed to eight million black people.[*4]

No, it is monopoly capitalism that has prospered from the exploitation of white workers as well as the super-exploitation of black workers. It is here that the onus of blame must be

---

* For a family of four, the level of income was $3,335 (non-farm). Source: U.S. Department of Commerce, Bureau of the Census, 1967.

placed. This is not to negate the fact that white workers, primarily through their racism, have, nearly always, uncompromisingly supported the corporate structure in the economic rape of black America. But it must be kept in mind that it is one thing to support and quite another to control. Mr. Muhammad's belief in the existence of an all-inclusive white United Front enjoying all the benefits of corporate capitalism's dominance is unsupportable in fact. And it can be assumed that if by some stretch of the imagination an economic program such as that put forth by the black elite could ever be implemented, there is little chance that black America would attain a genuine black United Front.

Outside of the newspaper *Muhammad Speaks,* which has grown in economic importance because of its cultural appeal to the black masses, the other business enterprises owned by the Nation are, practically speaking, of little economic importance to the welfare of black America. The types of businesses owned by the Nation are, as would be expected, in the traditional areas of black business concentration (small restaurants, grocery stores, barber shops, etc.). Although the businesses are collectively owned by the Nation, they are still run exclusively on the basis of providing a profit return. Under American capitalism, this automatically means maximum price levels. Collective ownership of businesses, then, means very little in this case. Instead of the private profit from the businesses benefiting one black owner, as is the case with most black businesses, it goes to a small group of private owners for their sole benefit. The operation here, in reality, differs little from the operation of the controlling corporations where the wealth is also concentrated. As Leo Huberman has pointed out:

> In capitalist society, things are cooperatively operated and cooperatively made, but they are not cooperatively owned by those who made them. Therein lies the fundamental contradiction in capitalist society—the fact that while production is social, the result of collective effort and labor, appropriation is private, individual.[4]

The best estimate of the Nation's income is that it grosses $500,000 or more yearly. It appears, though, that only a fraction of this comes from actual business investments. The Nation embarked on an extensive drive to open up new business enterprises in many black communities, particularly in the North. Even so, the volume of business done by Nation-owned enterprises is still comparatively small, by the general standards of business.

Undaunted by this, the Nation seems to be placing greater emphasis on expansion into new areas of business enterprise. This is especially true for the field of agricultural development. This comes at a time when the condition of the black farmer and farm worker has steadily deteriorated. More than 90 percent of the black farm workers and farmers are concentrated in the South. In 1960, their income averaged less than $4,000 per year; the latest figures place the median income of the black farmer at $3,992. In nearly a decade, the income of the black farmer has actually decreased. The situation has grown so critical that the black farmer has increasingly been forced to leave his land and migrate to some urban black ghetto in search of more rewarding work. The same pattern holds true for smaller farms belonging to white growers. For example, in 1960 there were 876,000 black and 5,520,000 white farmers and farm workers in the United States. As of 1967, the number of black farmers and farm workers had been reduced by 52 percent, to 423,000, while the number of white farm workers had similarly been cut by 31 percent to 3,131,000.[5]

The Nation seems to feel that its "back to the land" farm program can at least in part reverse this trend, and at the same time establish an independent black agricultural production line. Ultimately, it is thought that the Nation will be able to stock and supply its stores and restaurants with its own brand of food and products. But a realistic assessment of the present state of American agriculture shows that it will be very difficult to achieve this goal. Mechanization has already progressed to the point where the need for farm laborers has greatly diminished. It has been predicted in some circles that in the next few years the black farmer and farm worker will be entirely displaced from the land. Corporate industry and the government together are taking over most of the productive land, eliminating the small grower as a competitor. This, of course, explains the reason for the rapid decline in the income and the number of both black and white farmers. It is unlikely that the Nation, with its limited economic base, will under these conditions be in a position to break the monopoly that the government and the white corporate growers are increasingly gaining in the area of food growth and distribution.

No matter how hard the Nation pushes the concept of "Buy Black" or "self-help," a few small supermarkets or land holdings cannot alter the economic depression in black America. The era of the small businessman died over fifty years ago. It was killed by the emergence of corporate capitalism. The Nation, along with the black elite, has no real choice but to face this fact. The economic structure of America is so controlled that a pooling of black resources cannot reverse the trend which corporate capitalism has set in motion.

The launching of the Mississippi farm cooperative program shows this. This program was set up on 120 acres of land in Mississippi, under the direction of John Hatch and Andrew James. It was praised by *Muhammad Speaks* (November 22, 1968, p. 26) as an example of following the program of Mr. Muhammad. The farm cooperative program is a self-help venture by 900 farm families, who hope to turn their acres of land into a productive unit able to provide food for 12,000 people in Bolivar County, Mississippi. But to launch this program took $150,000 of Office of Economic Opportunity money. This certainly cannot be considered an instance of black self-help.

The hierarchy in the Nation, if it does let the organization evolve to the point where it begins a full-scale pursuit of the course of black capitalism, must be prepared to share responsibility with the black elite, which it continually denounces, for creating further divisions in the black communities. These divisions seem already to have appeared within the socioeconomic structure of the Nation, as they have in many other black organizations.

Employees in Nation-owned businesses are drawn from the ranks of the membership. From the scant information available, it seems that most of these employees are paid a wage in the form of what the Nation calls "charity." E. U. Essien-Udom, the Nigerian scholar, in his work *Black Nationalism*, cites a typical example: "A full-time employee, eighteen years of age, who works at one of the business establishments [of the Nation], gets $35 a week." [6]

Essien-Udom further points out that the Nation's employees have no right to collective wage bargaining. This eliminates one of the fundamental safeguards in any employee-owner relationship. Any true revolutionary movement which seeks to gain the needed mass base must always uphold the democratic principles of negotiation, criticism, and, most important of all, self-criticism in that organization's own internal structure. Some may argue that if one is talking about building a revolutionary movement there must be some temporary sacrifice. In both theory and practice, this is a very valid point. At the same time, one should not confuse a revolutionary movement, which black (and white) America truly needs, with a reform movement. For a revolutionary movement, the need for these principles is indisputable. A genuine national liberation movement, utilizing the varied methods of both class *and* race struggle, seeks to overturn the existing order in America. The Nation, through its emphasis on business development under the American system, does not seek to overturn, but instead to copy, thereby in effect supporting that system. However, if the Nation is, as it claims, moving toward the position of strengthening its ideal of black collective economic development, it must at least allow wage negotiation and collective bargaining for its member-employees. This is a right even America's corporate rulers grant on a minimal level to their employees. (Analysis of the contemporary American scene makes it necessary to allow for the deep-rootedness of white racism as a separate entity from the pure class analysis. This will be discussed later.)

In addition, the Nation is more than a movement in the traditional sense. To any of its members who have not yet developed a revolutionary perspective, the Nation represents a new way of life, with its own self-contained ends. The Nation, like its predecessors, moves under the "divine mission" concept. This image is combined with a program of black business development as being the true path for the liberation of black people. The finished result is the black nation.

By now, it is becoming obvious to some who sincerely believe that black people in the United States can build a black nation, that more serious thought must be given to other more suitable modes of economic production and distribution, modes that will not perpetuate the inequalities under which capitalism operates.

The Nation's five-point economic program is directly tied in with Mr. Muhammad's realization that America's corporate rulers are not about to give in to the long-standing demand of the Nation for a separate land. The land claim, as is widely known, has remained a central facet of the Nation's overall program. On the question of territorial separation, Mr. Muhammad has been consistent over the years. He has taken the position that the only solution to America's racial problem lies in the complete separation of black and white people. According to Mr. Muhammad, black people must be given fertile land, that is, mineral rich, by the former slave masters—read: the American ruling class. Further, the Nation feels that the new black nation should be supported by America's rulers for an unspecified period of time.

It should be noted here, just as an aside, that the ideal which recurs time and again throughout the pronouncements of many black "self-help" groups has appeared in the Nation's program. But it should be asked how blacks can call for black national independence from white America and in practically the same breath ask for material aid (more crumbs)? Either you are independent, which means self-supporting, or you are not; there is no middle ground. It is incorrect to equate self-help, as many nationalist groups have, *with* a corporate or government handout for some new black business. Or, as in the case of the Nationalist demands, for a separate black nation full of capitalist-operated black elite businesses.

It should also be noted that although there have been several earlier attempts by black men in America to secure a separate land for their people, Mr. Muhammad's proposal for a black nation marked the first time that a black nationalist leader expressed a desire for land within the United States. This represents an important shift in black philosophical perspective. For at last the two schools of thought, black economic development and black religious separatism, were tied together and committed to each other's growth on American soil. It had been the previous contention of all of the major black nationalist-separatist spokesmen, from Delaney through Garvey, that the black nation should be established in either Africa or South America. This would, they felt, require a mass black exodus from the shores of North America.

So we see that the Nation's economic program, with its heavy emphasis on business development, has, in the tradition of Garvey, been intimately related to, if not totally replaced by, its concept of black nationhood. This being the case, Essien-Udom has asked a very pertinent question and made a very pertinent observation: "Does Muhammad really expect the United States to offer Negroes land here in the Western Hemisphere ?... On the other hand, his real intention may be no more than to get Negroes to pool their resources for the purchase of property both in the cities and in the rural areas."[7] So as not to leave any doubt as to what economic system Mr. Muhammad feels closest to, Essien-Udom continues: "He is impressed with the great wealth of the United States AND SEES NO REASON WHY NEGROES HAVE TO GO ELSEWHERE TO LOOK FOR ANYTHING MORE."[8]

Also implied here is that Mr. Muhammad is using the land issue as a means for gathering new converts and building up the personal wealth of the Nation. If black nationhood is in fact no longer the ideal, then that is the inescapable conclusion, particularly since Mr. Muhammad himself owns some income property;

a few of his apartment buildings are rented to members of the
Nation. Thus he has a personal stake in American society.

At this juncture, the Nation's hierarchy has apparently satisfied
itself that it can create an independent black economy in coexistence with corporate capitalism. The reality of the situation is
that the Nation can little more hope to succeed in developing an
American black national economy than has the black elite. This
will remain the case despite the fact that the Nation possesses a
skillfully developed organizational structure and a higher degree
of cultural awareness than does the black elite.

What is worth noting here, and this truly compounds the situation, is that in the area of cultural awareness, the Nation, under
Mr. Muhammad's guidance, has made an enormous contribution
to the social awakening that the black masses are currently experiencing. The Nation, as most black people are by now aware, has
throughout its existence placed a total emphasis on the knowledge and understanding of the history and culture, past and
present, of the Islamic and African states. The Nation has combined this with an attempt to educate black people thoroughly on
the importance of their own history and culture, which is directly
related to that of the Third World nations.

Further, it can never be forgotten that the Nation shaped much
of the character and thought of the man who has become black
America's greatest source of inspiration, Malcolm X. In addition,
Muhammad Speaks, the news organ of the Nation, is in tone and
content one of the most revolutionary black newspapers in the
country. It has consistently upheld many of the principles of the
black liberation struggle. More coverage of current events can be
found in its pages than in any other black newspaper, where news
for the most part is slanted toward the American ruling elite, just
as it is in the white Establishment press.

While black people should respect the Nation for these practices, they must at the same time criticize the Nation for any failure
on its part to follow its progressive cultural program into the area
of economic theory. The Nation's potential for contributing to

the national liberation struggle in America is enormous, only if it can renounce any ties it might develop to the bankrupt sectarianism of black capitalist business development. Hopefully it will see that in the long run such a posture will serve to strengthen rather than break the economic stranglehold of the corporate structure on black America.

As some black thinkers have already pointed out, the issue is no longer how much land or how many stores the black elite is able to acquire. They, in fact, never will be able to compete on the same level with the American corporate structure. Building a black Westinghouse or U.S. Steel Corporation is completely out of the question at this time. The point is that *under the American economic structure black corporations could no more solve the mass employment needs of the black communities than white corporations.* Over the last decade, the unemployment rate for black people has been 10.7 percent of the civilian labor force, while the rate for white people has been 5.3 percent. This is a ratio of over 2 to 1. The above statement is justified entirely when it is considered that during this same period, the power of corporate capitalism has risen to unprecedented heights. A black corporation, like the white controlling corporations, cannot deal with the problems of black unemployment. In the dynamic of the American economy, it is absolutely essential that a reservoir of unemployed labor be maintained. Marx labeled this surplus pool of labor, which is a common feature of every capitalist economy, "the industrial reserve army."

It should also be clear that, given the pressures which govern the operation of American corporate business, a black corporate enterprise would be just as determined as a white to squeeze as much profit as possible out of the black working class, while only secondarily concerning itself with the welfare and problems of the black communities, if at all.

With this said, the economic programs put forth under the auspices of the black church should be seen as not simply impractical and unattainable, but very dangerous to pursue. At a time when the strength of the black masses needs to be built, many black religious sects are instead giving new life to the class which has faithfully served as a buffer for corporate capitalism within the black ghettos—the black middle class.

For example, the Nation issued directives to all its members opposing the wearing of Afro hairstyles, African robes, and inter-marriage with Muslims outside of the Nation. This should be viewed as a logical manifestation of the Nation's all-out attempt to identify directly with the mainstream of the American capitalist economy. Under these circumstances, continuing identification by the Nation with the cultural needs of the black masses has been deemed unwise. This has been the standard contention of the black elite over the years. The aim of the Nation then seems to be that of keeping its members isolated from the trends prevalent today in black America.

The Nation's stance has also created further problems of an organizational nature. Many black people who already consider themselves politically astute have been led by the actions of the Nation into viewing this as a step forward: They feel that it is a move on the part of the Nation to discipline and mold black people into a unified force for future struggle. It is indisputable that discipline is an integral part of any true revolutionary movement, but in the context of the Nation's present pursuits, instead of a unified force the black communities will create only a fragmented, ineffectual force.

Black-organized religion, for the sake of its own survival if nothing else, must reorient its political-economic philosophy. Of course, if this is done, the black church will be in a better position to align itself behind the true needs not only of the black masses in America, but of its class and race allies in the captive Third World.

— 3 —

Whose Capitalism?

The tendency toward concentration of wealth is, and has been for some time now, the single most powerful imperative in American society. If the new wave black-capitalist theoreticians doubt this, they should examine these figures closely: in 1904, out of 216,180 business enterprises in the United States, 1,900 of them (or 0.9 percent) had a yearly output valued at $1 million or more. These 1,900 enterprises together employed 1.4 million workers, or 25.6 percent of the 5.5 million in the workforce. Their output, taken together, was valued at $5.6 billion, or 38 percent of the total of $14.8 billion. This means that, in 1904, less than 1 percent of the business enterprises in the United States employed one-fourth of the American labor force while controlling some three-eighths of the output of all business enterprises.

By 1909, five years later, 3,060 business enterprises (or 1.1 percent of a total of 268,491) employed 2.2 million workers out of 6.6 million, or one-third of the total, while their combined annual output was valued at $9 billion out of $20.7 billion, or 43.5 percent of the total.[1]

According to a study made in 1953, by Robert Lampman for

the National Bureau of Economic Research, 1.6 percent of the adult population in America owned 32 percent of all privately owned wealth. This consisted of 82.2 percent of all stock, 100 percent of state and local (tax-exempt) bonds, 38.2 percent of federal bonds, 88.5 percent of other bonds, 29.1 percent of the cash, 36.2 percent of mortgages and notes, 13.3 percent of life insurance reserves, 5.9 percent of pension and retirement funds, 18.2 percent of miscellaneous property, 16.1 percent of real estate, and 22.1 percent of all debts and mortgages. This was the picture in 1953. In the years since, studies conducted in the area of wealth and economic control in America indicate that the trend toward the concentration of wealth and power has steadily increased.

Fortune magazine's yearly listing of the top 500 corporations in America in 1968 showed that these corporations accounted for 64 percent of all industrial sales in the United States. This is up 9 percent from a decade ago. Combined they employed 687 out of every 1,000 workers and accounted for 74 percent of the total profits. Even more, the top ten, in this order: General Motors, Standard Oil (N.J.), Ford, General Electric, Chrysler, IBM, Mobil Oil, Texaco, Gulf Oil, and U.S. Steel increased their earnings by 21 percent, or double the rate of all the other 490 companies. As *Time* magazine, one of corporate America's main organs, pointed out: "The trend of the 500 underscores the growing importance of 'economies of scale.'"

It is unnecessary at this point to go into any further analysis of the dynamic of capitalism. Competition, or "free enterprise," has given way to closed enterprise. This is the essence of monopoly capitalism. Corporate enterprises today only engage in "free enterprise" among themselves. Standard Oil and Shell Oil, General Motors and Ford Motors, compete to some extent, but even here power is in varying degrees intertwined. So it is utterly absurd to envision the corner grocery store matched against Safeway foods or a second-hand car dealer matched against Ford. Realizing this, corporate capitalism has chosen to move into the black communities on a greater scale. The cover-up continues to be the plea that the small black businessman must be helped along in his development. The game white corporate enterprise is playing is still the same, and the stakes are still to tighten up its control of the black communities *and to prevent future black rebellions.*

A *Ramparts* magazine story (June 29, 1968) pointed out that the *Harvard Business Review,* in discussing the black rebellions, laid the blame on the small businesses in the black communities. The article, which was titled "Better Deal for Ghetto Shoppers," went on to state: "High prices, shoddy goods and usurious credit are the inevitable consequences of the least efficient segment of the business community. To allow these Mom and Pop stores (traditional small ghetto grocery stores) to rebuild—if they have been burned out—and thus secure the ghetto market for themselves is just perpetuating the system that caused the unrest in the beginning. It will do more to aggravate the problem than relieve it."

American corporate enterprise, by virtue of the all-embracing economic base it possesses, is in a position to call the shots, so to speak, on every facet of the American economy. The consumer is, and is viewed as, a captive dumping ground for every com-modity the corporate power structure wishes to push. Small and new businesses are in a precarious position. And nowhere is this more true than in the case of the small merchant in the black community. The black consumer, provided he has transporta-tion, can go into the large white chain markets or department stores outside (and more and more, inside) the ghetto and buy nationally advertised products at comparatively low prices. Small businesses in the ghetto, both black and white, are, by virtue of their position, in no shape to match these businesses on the level of pricing. Corporate enterprise deals in huge inventories and volume, thereby gaining the advantage of lower pricing while still reaping enormous profits. This is part of the vicious cycle of cor-porate enterprise's control of the market.

For example, can one imagine a small meat market in the black community directly importing for its own exclusive use beef from Argentina? Of course not. But a corporate chain market, such as A&P, is able to operate its own cattle-breeding ranches in Argentina. This enables them to avoid the costs involved in paying separately a breeder, middleman, and importer for the beef which they stock in their stores. By performing the function of all three, it is easy to see how a corporate chain market is able to undercut price levels continually. The consequent loss of business forces the small market to cut down on buying and selling. This is the cycle of the marginal business, which more often than not collapses economically.

The small black businessman is thus doubly victimized by corporate capitalism. Apart from his generally unsuccessful attempts to compete with corporate enterprise, he is still a black consumer.

The pattern is clear for those who want to see. The corporate structure destroys the small businessman through its daily operations in the marketplace, while at the same time it maintains a pretense of helping the black businessman.

Thus the corporate power structure has in recent months set up councils in New York and Detroit for the ostensible purpose of "economic development" in the black ghetto. Some of the largest corporations in America, such as Mobil Oil, Metropolitan Life Insurance, General Motors, U.S. Steel, and Westinghouse, to name a few, are participating in planning and guidance. Many of America's business leaders are actively involved, including such notables as Andrew Heiskell, chairman of Time Incorporated, the ever present Henry Ford II, chairman of the Ford Motor Co., and David Rockefeller of the Chase Manhattan Bank.

So as not to leave any illusions, Ford perhaps best summed up corporate capitalism's sentiments in a speech delivered at Yale University: "It is clearly in the self-interest of businessmen to enlarge their markets by selling housing, insurance, credit, restaurant meals, haircuts, automobiles and all other products and services to all comers on equal terms." Ford continued: "In short, the profit motive provides abundant incentive for businessmen to help solve the economic problems of the disadvantaged."

These individuals and their multibillion-dollar corporations are cooperating with the established national civil rights leaders, Roy Wilkins of the NAACP and Whitney Young of the Urban League, in the development of their programs. This follows what has been the accepted pattern over the years, and these two organizations have been particularly adept in their capacity as hired frontmen for America's ruling elite.

The corporate power structure, however, has realized that these men are rapidly being discredited as leaders in the black communities. To get around that, the corporate power structure has found it convenient, while still retaining its ties to the old-line leaders, to work with many of the newer "grassroots" organizations in black America. Corporate enterprise has correctly perceived that these organizations and leaders, many of which have sprung up directly after each black rebellion in area after area, are in closer touch with the needs and aspirations of the black workers.

Included in this category of new black community organizations are, of course, many of the so-called black nationalist groups. The corporate switch to these new groups has been necessitated precisely because of the militance of black workers. It is clear that if control is to be maintained, the tactics of five years ago can't be used today. Capitalism, to protect and increase its interests, is capable of assuming many forms, running the gauntlet from fascist repression to liberal co-optation. At this point, the latter form is being tried in relation to black America. Lyle M. Spencer, president of Science Research Associates (a subsidiary of IBM), has aptly summed up this new situation: "The military-industrial complex" is about to be superseded by a "social-industrial complex." [2]

And just who are these new leaders and organizations that make up the social end of this "complex"? The list is very long.

But perhaps the newest black organization that fits the description of combining black capitalist pursuits with a black nationalist verbal orientation is CORE (Congress of Racial Equality).

CORE, under the direction of Roy Innis, was one of the first organizations to back the plan of President Nixon for black capitalism.*[5] Over the past two years CORE has gone through a dramatic programmatic shift. It started out as a "non-violent" demonstration-geared organization, but it has moved steadily to its current position of advocating the creation of a black national economy, which is diametrically opposite to the stance of "integration." This to a large degree explains CORE's support of Nixon's plan. But it doesn't explain its inability to see the contradictions inherent in its new view.

CORE and the other black "nationalist" organizations that are promoting Nixon's line feel that in order for an independent black economy to survive it must be patterned after the American corporate structure. Instead of demanding integration into a white office or neighborhood, these organizations are trying to integrate into the whole economic system. This represents nothing more than carrying the phony concept of integration, which these organizations denounce, from the individual level to the group level. This is, in fact, the position taken by Dr. Nathan Wright, chairman of the Newark Black Power Conference of 1967. Wright, in his book *Black Power and Urban Unrest,* advocates black unity as a means of *gaining entrance into every level of American society.* As he explains: "Undoubtedly the most strategic opportunity which our American capitalistic system has to preserve or strengthen itself lies in the possibility of providing

* Richard Nixon, in a speech on April 25, 1968, said: "By providing technical assistance and loan guarantees, by opening new capital sources, we can help Negroes to start new businesses in the ghetto and to expand existing ones." Nixon called for the creation of a bank to finance business enterprises in poverty areas; increased Small Business Administration loans; management training courses; and tax incentives for corporate business enterprises that locate in the ghetto areas. *U.S. News & World Report,* September 30, 1968, p. 65.

the Negro community with both a substantial and an immediate stake in its operation at every level. The Black Power thrust is toward the unity of black people for the good of the whole nation."

As with the old-line black elite, these new wave black nationalist organizations have little historical understanding of American capitalism. Roy Innis himself is an excellent example. He stated: "Production and wealth are made by two factors, labor and capital. We have been cut in on the labor portion of it but never on the capital part. The real rewards are in the capital."[3] Mr. Innis is undoubtedly right when he says that ownership of capital is the key to economic power. Capital, however, is not something that is just gotten out of the air. Capital is produced by labor. In America this labor, especially that of black workers, has produced the capital and wealth for the few giant controlling corporations. They are the ones, and the only ones, who have grown richer as the result. And the labor pool on which they have successfully capitalized daily grows larger. Mr. Innis obviously does not realize that this is something that has been built into the American economic system.

Innis has CORE going all-out to try and make black capitalism a reality. At a bankers conference in Chicago, he demanded that the banks turn over $6 billion in reparations for black business development. In another effort, CORE has chosen to work with the leading corporate brokerage firm, Shearson, Hammill, & Co., in a plan for Harlem business development. Shearson, as part of its agreement with CORE, has promised that *some* of the profits gained from its initial investment in Harlem will go toward the establishment of an independent foundation for black business guidance and support. CORE's former chief, Floyd B. McKissick, apparently taking the same cue, has opened Floyd B. McKissick Enterprises, Inc., in New York. McKissick has run frequent ads in the *Muhammad Speaks* classified business section.

McKissick's position is in some respects paradoxical. In his book, *3/5 of a Man*, he sharply attacks the whole American socioeconomic system, but then confusedly turns around to give a conflicting interpretation of an historical problem: "By not providing economic opportunity for the former slaves, America missed the one chance to absorb black people into the economic system. By developing black capitalists at an early date, capitalism could have bought a great deal of time with a comparatively small investment." From this he develops his major thesis: "Ownership of businesses in the ghetto must be transferred to black people, either individually or collectively. . . . Attached to this program can be the 'communiversity' or other training agencies where black people can be taught to operate various types of businesses."

Even the supposedly "militant" black nationalist magazine *Liberator* has gotten into the act here. The magazine's editor-in-chief, Dan Watts, in what could be construed as a tacit endorsement of the candidacy of Nixon during the last election, wrote in an editorial: "Either major candidate [referring to Humphrey, Nixon, and Wallace] would be acceptable if he agreed 'convincingly,' to fulfill our [black people's] demands. At the moment, Nixon would seem to have the edge, as he is at least 'talking' about Black Power and economics."[4] Behind the charade and pretense is the belief of corporate enterprise that the black ghetto can be made into a potential long-term source of even greater private profit. This is not to deny the fact that it is important for the corporate structure to maintain control, but to make a profit is still their number one priority. U.S. Gypsum and Litton Industries are two current examples of this. Both corporations are in the process of undertaking research and development projects on newer building materials and techniques which more directly appeal to the black ghetto market. Richard Cloward and Frances Piven note here that "there is the promise of profit to be made in removing poverty. Redevelopment promises to be a huge business, running into billions of dollars."[5]

The old-line black elite, which by no means has been forgotten, also stands to gain from the machinations of corporate enterprise.

Their businesses are also due to be promoted just as vigorously as in the past. New funds are to be allocated for existing black businesses, for it is still felt by the corporate power structure that "established" black business can serve as an immediate front image. As it stands now, there is no threat here whatsoever of another competitive force.

With this brief background of recent developments, the question that now forcefully presents itself is: What is the actual position of black capitalism today?

Since the NNBL was founded by Booker T. Washington in 1900, approximately twenty national black business associations have sprung into existence. These associations cover nearly every area of black business. They range from the Amalgamated Publishers, Inc., which is the national representative for some sixty black newspapers, to the International Florists Association, Inc., which has a membership of 300 black florists.[6]

In Philadelphia in 1964, the Drexel Institute of Technology conducted a large-scale study of small businesses. The study found thirteen small black manufacturing enterprises operative. Of this number, eight were beauty-product manufacturing companies and two were clothing manufacturers. Thus out of the thirteen, ten were still in the traditional areas of black business concentration. Further, although black businesses made up 9 percent of all the businesses in the city, nearly all of them were in the retail and service trade fields, which again are the lowest paying categories of business. A full 35 percent of the black businesses were either barber, or beauty shops, two of the most non-vital areas of business concern. And the overwhelming majority (77 percent) of these businesses were located in the black community, while at the same time better than half of the businesses operated in the black community were white-owned. For the black businesses, median sales ranged from $2,500 for beauty shops to $6,800 for luncheonettes.[7]

It should be added that these findings are inconsistent with those that have been obtained on a national basis. According to SBA figures, only 3 percent of all businesses in America are owned by non-whites. In the Watts section of Los Angeles, 98 percent of all the businesses are owned by white people. This is a more normative example than Philadelphia. In addition, *Time* magazine (October 18, 1968, p. 98) has estimated that only one out of every thousand black persons in America owns a business, whereas for whites it is one out of every forty. Philadelphia, then, has both a higher number and a higher median of "prosperity" for its black businesses than any other urban area in the country. (Harlem, in New York, might be thought to be the only exception to this, but it is estimated that in Harlem anywhere from 80 to 95 percent of the businesses are owned by whites.) This has prompted Eugene Foley to write: "The types and character of Negro business have not changed greatly since Du Bois wrote *The Philadelphia Negro* in 1899."[8]

This, as can be seen, is no mean exaggeration of the evidence. If anything, Foley's statement does not go far enough. The fact is that not only has there been no substantial change in either the type or character of black business, but there has also been no significant increase in the proportionate volume of business done by these black firms. Comparatively speaking, when all factors are taken into consideration, such as cost of living, growth of corporate enterprise, shift in black population, etc., there has been an actual decline in the importance of black business over the last fifty years. For example, between 1950 and 1960, it was noted that the number of black-owned restaurants and retail outlets actually decreased by one-third.[9] Since then their number has probably declined even further, as a result of the increased pressure placed on them by the growth and popularity of the white-owned chain drive-in restaurants and stands (McDonald's hamburgers, Jack-in-the-Box drive-ins, etc.) as well as such "low-cost" department stores as Woolworth's, Grant's, and so on. These enterprises, as a result of domestic corporate imperialism, are beginning to move into the black communities in ever greater numbers.

As for the vital areas of commerce and trade, Harding Young

has stated: "There are, however, almost no Negro owned or managed manufacturing, transportation, or wholesaling businesses, and there are few corporations of any kind."[10] Taken collectively, at this point, the capital from all of the black-owned businesses in the United States would not equal one-half of 1 percent of the nation's total.[11]

This figure corresponds for banks as well. According to Berkeley G. Burrell, president of the National Business League, black banks, with their total assets combined, equal less than one-half of 1 percent of the total assets of the Bank of America alone.

Further underscoring this, Dempsey J. Travis, president of the Sivart Mortgage Corporation, a black-owned firm, revealed that the number of black businesses has declined dramatically over the past forty years. Travis, speaking before a recent meeting of the United Mortgage Bankers of America, a small organization composed of some fifty black businessmen, stated: "It seems that the development of black capitalism within any period—dating back to the post–Civil War days—has depended greatly on the mood and climate of the power structure."

It is often heard today that black businesses are in a much better position to give employment to black people. The figures on employment for black business tell an entirely different story. In the combined areas of banking, finance, real estate, and insurance—the black elite's so-called field of economic breakthrough—black businesses employed 5,000 people in 1960, or 1.1 percent of the 413,000 persons who worked in these areas across the nation. For the other areas, such as construction, manufacturing, utilities, etc., the percentage of the total was below 1 percent. Only in the fields of retail trade and the services, the most menial, was there any increase (to 2.5 percent).[12]

Along with this, black businessmen have an unemployment rate nearly three times as high as that of white businessmen. (It seems that black businessmen are having a hard time employing themselves, let alone black workers.) Eighty percent of black businessmen earn less than $5,000 a year, whereas 60 percent of white businessmen earn over $5,000. Why the failure? Endless excuses and explanations have been offered both by the black elite and its mentors in the white corporate power structure, in an attempt to get at (or at times to cover up) the causes. Examples abound throughout the voluminous reports and studies the myth-makers of black business have conducted. The blame for black business failure for a long time was laid on black people themselves. The main arguments can be easily summarized: black proprietors are inefficient, lazy, lack education, have little business experience, are slow and discourteous. At various times each or all of these have been mentioned. Frazier cites one of the typical surveys. Here it was "found" that 46 percent of the black consumers interviewed said they were dissatisfied with black businesses because the operators were too slow; 44 percent said the operators were careless; 23 percent said they were discourteous; and 29 percent said they were inefficient.[13] But these complaints are, if anything, symptomatic effects rather than causes. Black businesses fail because the very economic system in which they are trying to succeed is stacked against them.

The new programs that are being suggested or implemented for correcting this situation reflect the stake that corporate capitalism has in the continuation of this structure. Among the programs that could be included in this class are the "domestic development bank," a plan which permits small businessmen to borrow capital from various corporate-government agencies. In New York, Governor Rockefeller has proposed the establishment of an Urban Redevelopment Corporation, which would serve as sort of a coordinating agency between state, local, and federal agencies to ensure the investment of both private funds and industry in the ghetto. In Baltimore, the Ford Foundation has partially funded a program called the Council for Economic Business Opportunity. These are just two examples of what corporate capitalism has on the drawing boards for black America. In nearly every major city a program or organization has come into existence, almost always after a "riot," with the aim of building black business, and more particularly corporate industry, into a viable entity within the black communities. The black elite and the corporate power structure, the primary beneficiaries of these programs, anxiously—or more to the point, greedily—anticipate the construction of a national system of black capitalist enterprise, which, by necessity, would be totally dependent, regardless of the black elite's pronouncements, on corporate enterprise for its economic life.

Another agency that figures heavily in the schemes of corporate enterprise is the Small Business Administration (SBA). For a short period it was thought that the SBA held out a promise of hope for black business development. Between 1954 and 1964 very few SBA loans went to black businesses. Since 1964, however, the SBA has granted more than 2,000 loans to black businesses. The optimism that sprang up around the role of the SBA in black business development has largely dissipated. In an interview in *U.S. News & World Report* of September 30, 1968, Howard J. Samuels, then SBA administrator, admitted that his agency's loan program was proving to be a failure. Another SBA spokesman said in the same article: "These loans are showing a high failure rate—about double the regular rate, and this rate will probably rise. Not all of these loans are to Negroes, but many of them are. So, from this you can assume that the failure rate of Negro loans will be higher than the present overall loss rate." It is useful to note that the great majority of the SBA's loans were to black businesses in the standard areas of enterprise—"soul food" restaurants, beauty shops, etc.—that by now appear to be reserved for black businessmen.

Because of policy measures, SBA loans going to black businesses that want to expand into more vital areas of commerce and trade are extremely hard, if not impossible, to obtain. From March 1, 1967, to April 30, 1968, only thirty-six loans over $50,000 were made by the SBA to black businesses. This situation has prompted many of the leading spokesmen for the interests of the black elite to decry publicly black people's lack of interest in major industry. For example, Berkeley G. Burrell, president of the NBL, chided black businessmen for seeking petty loans of $5,000 and $10,000 from the SBA. Burrell feels that black people must start thinking big and start planning shopping centers instead of the usual grocery stores and chicken stands. He feels that this is the only way white people will begin to respect black people. Burrell declared: "Negroes will be able to deal with white people when they can sit across the table millionaire to millionaire."[14]

In Mr. Burrell's remarks we see the embodiment of the NBL's seventy-year legacy of misdirection and failure. For this is truly, in every respect, an astounding statement for a supposedly aware black man to make. Burrell is apparently not ready to acknowledge the fact that even though there are already a small number of black millionaires in the country, they are still looked upon in America as "niggers." It is not just a simple question of an individual black man possessing wealth or power. All the money or power in the world wouldn't have saved Malcolm X, Medgar Evers, or Martin Luther King from the assassins' bullets in America. It is a system—capitalist exploitation and oppression—rather than an individual that has institutionalized, over a period of 400 years, racism into white America's body politic. There is no way around the fact that capitalism and racism are bound in America tighter than the Gordian knot.

Further, one may wonder if Burrell has asked himself the question: From whom are these black millionaires going to make their millions? I think the answer is fairly obvious—the black worker, who else?

The justification the black elite uses for pushing its program of business development is that this is a means for keeping the money in the community. This is of course a totally fallacious, unthinkingly mouthed cliché. For it to have any basis at all it must first be proven that the black elite identifies first and foremost with the masses in the black communities. And as has already been demonstrated, the first impulse of a member of the black elite, be he businessman or professional, once he gets a little money or status, is to leave his community, if not physically then psychologically. As Carmichael and Hamilton have observed:

> The goals of integrationists are middle-class goals, articulated primarily by a small group of Negroes with middle-class aspirations or status. Their kind of integration has meant that a few blacks "make it.". . . Those token Negroes—absorbed into a white mass—are of no value to the remaining black masses.[15]

Carmichael and Hamilton are absolutely correct. But unfortunately they haven't gone far enough. It is often the case when members of the black elite do remain in the black community, as most black businessmen do, that it is not for the purpose of incorporating their skills and talents into the struggles of the black masses, but to increase their own personal wealth.

A concrete example will serve to illustrate. Hobart Taylor, Sr., is a black millionaire. According to his estimate, he is worth $5 million. Taylor started out in Houston, Texas, with an insurance business and later expanded by purchasing a taxi franchise. He initially established his economic base in the black community; he even admits that he was in an almost totally segregated business. This alone, however, wasn't the determining factor in his success. He got credit and financing from Houston banks only through the intercession of a white friend. And where does he stand today? As one might expect, his first identification is with capitalism and private profit: "I talk to white businessmen a lot, too. I tell them it's just not profitable to keep the Negro ignorant. We need know-how folks paying taxes and not ignorant ones on relief."

Whether Taylor knows it or not, he let out more truth in this statement than he probably intended when he referred to white businessmen reaping greater profits from the economic advancement of black people. The theory is: the more money made, the greater the potential for exploitation. This statement further reinforces the contention that the corporate power structure has an ulterior motive—private profit—in pushing black capitalism. Finally, to show just what Taylor, the black millionaire whose praises Burrell sings, thinks of black unity (at best a minimal program) and militancy: "If all those [white] business houses would advertise prominently that they're hiring Negroes, it would give all Negroes hope. And it would kill off the Stokely Carmichaels."[16]

This underscores an important point: Black capitalism or white capitalism, black millionaire or white millionaire, black corporate head or white corporate head, under American capitalism allegiance is first and last to business and private profit. Any rocking of the boat will be opposed just as quickly by the black elite as it is by the white corporate power structure.

One of the cardinal principles of the latter-day black economic nationalists is insistence on a program of black "self-help." One of the leading proponents of this line is Dr. Thomas W. Matthew, a neurosurgeon. Dr. Matthew currently heads an organization which, quite appropriately, is titled NEGRO (National Economic Growth and Reconstruction Organization). Matthew, in an interview in *U.S. News & World Report* (July 22, 1968), stated: "We cannot have real integration until we have integration of equals." Undoubtedly this is true. But Matthew is of course speaking from the same theoretical posture as Burrell ("millionaire to millionaire"). Matthew continues by equating economic independence with economic power. As a step in achieving black unity and a reshaping of black thought, this would be acceptable. But even here, Matthew, like many of the other black elite "theoreticians," is confused over the means and ends for implementing this program. When questioned as to the role of the federal government, Matthew had this to say: "We have proposed to Congress a plan under which the government would lend annually up to 100 million dollars at 2 percent interest and would guarantee private loans at 4 percent to promote black business enterprises."

Thus on the one hand Matthew contends that black people can attain economic independence through their own efforts; on the other, he negates his argument by assigning to the government the role of major supporter. Matthew doesn't even bother to spell out how long this "domestic colonialism" is supposed to last. All he can say is "annually."

That Matthew is looking for a personal profit goes without saying. He says that he wants good, productive workers (translated: hard work—low pay). "Those industries make the profit for us, and we use the true free-enterprise system." Matthew, then, will accept the system of capitalism and its "myth of free enterprise" and at the same time work for an independent black economic base.

But Matthew, in reality, couldn't possibly want the latter. For the end result of his program will not ultimately lead to any black economic independence, but to a greater share in the capitalist system—thus to integration.

Another proponent of black business, the Reverend Leon Sullivan of Philadelphia, has adopted a similar position. Dr. Sullivan, the leading figure behind the Zion Investment Corporation which established Philadelphia's first black-developed shopping center, Progress Plaza, had this to say: "The government can and should give significant help in providing credit and other financial support for black-initiated and black-run enterprises of any size. Perhaps there will be large banks supported by federal funds to help things along. But I believe that such help is our minor resource, and that the major factor must be the involvement of private enterprise." (*U.S. News & World Report,* February 17,1969.)

But this is by no means the complete picture. The emergence of black pride and consciousness on the part of many in the black communities has given the black elite more and varied opportunities to profit from these new developments. There has been, for example, a noticeable increase over the past two years in the number of "new breed" enterprises. The primary concern of these businesses is to capitalize, in the clothing market, on the design and sale of the latest in "African" fashions. These fashions are usually imitative and cheap, without any real concern for authenticity, styles you would be likely to find on a Hollywood Tarzan set rather than any place in Africa. And, of course, these garments are usually sold at the highest price possible. These "new breed" black businessmen wonder why black people choose to go to the large white department stores to buy their "African" apparel. A recent advertisement in a Los Angeles newspaper announced the sale of an "African" wedding dress for $5.99 at the May Company department store. This same dress, made from the same material and design, if bought at one of the numerous "African" apparel shops operated by black businessmen in Los Angeles's black community, would cost between $10 and $20.

Similarly, Magnificent Natural Products, Inc., run by ex-barber Dennis Taylor, has, with the aid of the Ford Foundation, begun to be a top money-making operation, producing "natural" hair sprays for the popular Afro hairstyles. In this case, the assistance that was given by the Ford Foundation was channeled through the Negro Industrial and Economic Union (NIEU), an organization started by Jim Brown and several other black football players that is supposedly dedicated to the development of black business. The organization was given new life by a $520,000 grant from the Ford Foundation.

The black politician also plays a willing accomplice to the intrigues of the corporate power structure and the black elite. It has been through the black politician that these two forces have gained an easier access to the financial resources of the black masses. Augustus Hawkins, California's only black legislator in Washington, joined the chorus of those singing the praises of black business when he stated: "The need for expanded black entrepreneurship in our communities is long overdue." Hawkins also feels that the economic problems facing the black communities can be alleviated by "expanding the black capital base." He then comes to the expected conclusion: "Federal and private efforts must be multiplied many-fold. The average black businessman needs all of the supportive assistance available." [17]

In Cleveland, one can see the related pattern with the election of Carl Stokes as that city's first black mayor. The Warner & Swasey Co., which according to *Time* magazine "has a reputation for conservatism," recently decided to "assist" a black machine-tool firm, the C & B Machine Co., in its faltering operations. To illustrate how corporate imperialism works, out of 2,000 shares in this firm, two hundred were allotted to its director, Robert L. Coles, and the remaining shares went to Warner & Swasey. Meanwhile, Stokes continues to implore Cleveland's white businessmen to "invest" in the black community's "development." Almost without exception, in every black community where black faces—never confuse this with black power, as *Ebony* magazine apparently has—have begun to appear for the first time in the political arena, similar developments can be seen.

By contrast, Georgia legislator Julian Bond has of all black politicians taken the most realistic position on the role of corporate business and the black community: "Black capitalism seems to be an insurance policy offered by big business: 5 percent down so 95 percent won't be burned down." Bond, in an interview, put his finger squarely on the problem when he stated: "Business in the black community is desirable but the ownership of that business is crucial. I think the nature of capitalistic enterprises is that a larger group does the work, while the profits go into the pocket of a very few."

The new alignment of the black politician, the black businessman (old black elite), and elements of "new wave" black nationalists has formed a new vested-interest power base in the black communities. Working hand-in-hand with corporate enterprise, this neo-black elite is rapidly transforming the once expressive (and potentially revolutionary) cry of the black masses for black control of the black communities into *black capitalist control of the black communities.* This only reaffirms the American ethic that everything is expendable, including principle. Everything from nail polish to black nationalism can be, and is, hustled as long as there is a prospect for private profit.

It appears, then, that the interests of black workers, like those of white workers under American capitalism, are fast being lost in the mad shuffle of the neo-black elite to gain a personal "piece of the action" in exploitation. Black "self-help," or more accurately black *elite* "self-help," is simply boiling down to building up a few black businesses to the point where they would be in a position to pay, at best, a few black workers at $1.25 an hour or maybe with a little luck the minimum standard wage. This neat little arrangement for the neo-black elite offers absolutely no future for the national liberation of workers in America. There is no value in trading in white corporate exploitation for black exploitation.

—— 4 ——

Black Capitalism's Other Faces

As already mentioned, there has been a pronounced shift in emphasis on the part of the black masses from the limited goals of "civil rights" and "integration" to the more meaningful end of black liberation and human rights. A new search for ideas and approaches to deal with the problems confronting black America has accompanied this. Nevertheless, the plaguing tendency in the formulation of programs by even the most sincerely militant black leaders, is still to think in terms of relating in some way to the American system. The black leadership, for the most part, still labors under the misassumption that the American system can somehow be used, or, to borrow a popular phrase, "made more responsive." As an example, Jesse Jackson, leader of the black capitalist–oriented "Operation Breadbasket" in Chicago, is a practitioner of this type of patent nonsense. Jackson states: "Modern capitalism must become an instrument for a much wider base of participation on the part of the masses in the economic benefits of the nation."[1] The sentiment expressed here is quite noble, but the fact remains that if Mr. Jackson is talking about the masses participating in the economic benefits of the nation, then he certainly can't have capitalism in

mind. For if what Mr. Jackson wants were to ever come true, capitalism in America would be destroyed. But, as should be clear
from this, America, whether consciously or unconsciously, is
being used as a reference model by nearly every ideological segment of the black leadership.'

There have been other concepts suggested, however, by some
of the new black leaders, which at first glance appear to be a radical departure from the standard economic programs for the black
communities. These concepts can roughly be broken down into
three categories: (1) rebate plans, (2) economic cooperatives, and
(3) reparations—both financial and land claims.

The rebate plan is a relatively new idea. It is considered by
the few black leaders who have proposed it to be a practical,
financially workable method of economic development in the
black communities. Basically, the rebate plan calls for the merchants in the black communities to reinvest part of the profits
they make from the community into some community project,
such as a nursery, playground, or similar facility. It is felt that
this is the best way to prevent the merchants, both black and
white, from taking the profits exploited from black workers out
of the community. But the rebate plan should be unacceptable
to those in the forefront of the struggle for black liberation, precisely because it supports what black workers should be against:
namely, exploitative or private profit. The rebate plan obviously
accepts the basic premise of the American economic system.

Carmichael and Hamilton exemplify this. In *Black Power,* they
have laid down what to them is a plausible community rebate
plan. They feel that the black communities should organize and
boycott any merchants who refuse to go along with this program.
According to them, any merchant operating in the black community should be prepared to "reinvest" 40 to 50 percent of their
profits in that community. They are apparently prepared to allow
merchants who are busily engaged in the economic plunder of
the black communities to keep up their activities as long as they
agree to share a certain percentage of the spoils with the black

community. As one observer put it, "You let these merchants keep *only* 50 to 60 percent of their exploitation." Through years of shoddy economic practices, black people have more than paid for these business enterprises. Any plan that would permit or increase the economic subjugation of the black communities (as in practice the rebate plan would) is, at the least, unrealistically conceived.

Carmichael and Hamilton, by thus giving approval to the present structure of ghetto economics—i.e., the merchants' exploitation of black workers—reveal a certain unawareness regarding basic capitalist economic practice.

There is also the danger that the rebate plan could serve as a device by which the merchants in the black communities are given a way out of their present dilemma. An enterprising merchant could accept such a plan as a co-optative gesture which could turn around demands on the part of black workers for total control over their communities. Practically speaking, genuine control by black people over the institutions in their communities would run totally counter to any rebate plan. The illusion of shared power, which is what this plan represents, is no replacement for total power and control.

Secondly, it is thought in some quarters that a system of black cooperatives can be made a functional counter-balance to capitalism. This is by far the most positive proposal that has been offered. The only problem with it is that it has not dealt adequately with the whole question of corporate capitalism's economic dominance of America. A black cooperative enterprise, under capitalism, would still be subject to all the pressures—price levels, competition, acquisition of capital, maintenance of credit bases, etc.—that are experienced by the standard black business enterprise.

It should perhaps be noted here that the idea of a black cooperative economic system is certainly not a new one. The "mutual aid" societies in the Northern black communities in the eighteenth century, discussed earlier, were originally conceived as a step in this direction. However, as was pointed out, this ideal soon got lost with the emergence of the black elite and their subsequent development of a capitalist merchant-class perspective.

Du Bois, in the early part of the twentieth century, also gave expression to the idea of the black cooperative. In his second autobiography, *Dusk of Dawn,* he laid out what he considered to be a very comprehensive program for the total economic reconstruction of black America. His program dealt with nearly every aspect of economic life in the black communities, and included specific proposals for the collective organization of such groups as the black merchants, professionals, and workers. Du Bois noted then the basic class structure that characterized black America. He also recognized that the divisions which existed centered around the difference in outlook of each grouping. After acknowledging the pressing need for a decent standard of living, he warned black people not to "return to the old patterns of economic organization in America and the world:" He went further and explained that if black people continued in the direction they were headed, they would run the risk of creating a "Negro capitalist class which will exploit both Negro and white labor."

After making this incisive analysis and coming to the correct conclusion that the black ghettos would be around for a long time, Du Bois faltered and began to view these ghettos as a productive market that could be developed by black people. Here, of course, he differed from the black elite in the sense that he felt the black consumer market in the ghetto should be developed by the black consumers themselves, collectively and for their benefit, while the black elite sought to exploit the black consumer market in the ghetto for their own personal ends and profit.

The views of the black elite and Du Bois were both based on the naive premise that a large group of people in a particular area can rely on themselves alone to provide for all of their needs. This theory has collapsed in practice time and time again. It is impossible, as the economic system in America is constituted, to live in a detached vacuum. The black ghettos in America are not underdeveloped, which is how they are viewed, but overexploited.

The "cooperative commonwealth" Du Bois envisioned has been tried in some areas of the country and has failed. For example, an early study conducted by H. Naylor Fitzhugh, *Negroes in Consumer Cooperatives*, secured information on eleven cooperatives in seven states and seven cooperatives in the District of Columbia. Out of the seven in the District, only one which had been operating five years had a capital outlay of more than $5,000 and weekly sales amounting to $4,000. Ten of the cooperatives outside of the District did an annual volume of business of less than $10,000. It is interesting to note that the eleventh, the exception, was the Georgia State College Cooperative Association in Savannah. This was a combination bookstore, cafeteria, grocery and clothing store, and a confectionery. The annual volume of business was $25,000. This could be attributed largely to the fact that it was located on a black college campus, where many of the students lived and worked. This enterprise thus had a near-captive market.[2]

It was significant, even though in the wrong context, that Du Bois utilized in bold detail the basic principles of socialism rather than capitalism as the model for his plan. But as some cooperatives are designed today, the private profit motive is strongly operative. As such, a black cooperative without the necessary transformation of capitalism is just another method which the black elite has at its disposal for exploiting the black worker.

Before continuing, though, it must be said that this is not to imply that a system of black cooperatives is something to be dismissed. A program of cooperative economic planning can, even under the limitations corporate capitalism would place upon it, serve as an instrument for attacking some of the root economic problems that black people face. In fact, a beginning here is already being made in the South. The Southwest Alabama Farmers Cooperative Association (SWAFCA) is an excellent model. William Harrison, SWAFCA's director, explains just how sound cooperative planning can, in this instance, benefit the black farmer: "If fifty black farmers pool their money for fertilizer, they can purchase it by carloads, distribute it among themselves, and knock out the middleman, saving fifty dollars each." Harrison continues:

Five hundred black farmers can pool their money to get machinery and trucks and each one uses the equipment in turn. Therefore, the white man—and it's almost invariably a white man—who ordinarily rents out the machinery is eliminated, and the saving of each black farmer often is enough to pay for the equipment within a few years.

The third "school" of black economic thought has pushed the demand upon the federal government for reparations. As a take-off on the theme of the Nation, it is contended here that the white ruling class in America owes black people some form of compensation for their forced labor. Reparations are usually demanded in the form of money or land.

The whole question of reparations, if approached simply as a tactic for claiming the debt that America owes black people, would not be either a political or economic issue in the black communities. Reparations are in reality a very legitimate demand which black people are entitled to make. For building much of white America's wealth, black people have gotten only white racism and capitalist exploitation and oppression in return. Furthermore, there are legal as well as historical precedents set by various governments in this area. To illustrate, today West Germany pays reparations to Israel for the Nazi victimization of the Jews in Europe during World War II. Also, Finland paid Russia reparations up until 1944. The United States has paid reparations to Japanese-Americans for property stolen from them during their confinement in United States concentration camps during the war, and to both American Indians and the Philippines.

However, this issue has been taken up and voiced mostly by elements of the neo-black elite. The feeling is that if financial reparations are received this will somehow stimulate the growth of black business. This is their first concern. The case of the *Los Angeles Herald-Dispatch* exemplifies this point. The *Herald-Dispatch,* a black elite newspaper, has over a period of years continually pushed the demand for financial reparations from the federal government. At the same time, the *Dispatch* has proclaimed in front-page coverage that "the ownership of business is the last great hope for black Americans."[3] The *Dispatch* devotes a section of every edition to black businesses in Los Angeles. One of its main emphases is "Buy Black."

Financial reparations, employed for the purpose of supporting business, could serve as a main cog in the black elite's design to control the black communities. Even more, the reparations effort is nothing but another version of the neo-black elite's campaign to obtain corporate funds for black business. The *Dispatch* says: "Economic independence makes the man." It should quickly be submitted here that demanding financial reparations, like seeking money from corporate enterprise for black business development, will to the contrary not make the independent man (or people) but the dependent—or worse, dominated—man. The government is not going to channel money into the black communities without various stipulations on how it is to be used and who it's going to be used by. There is little doubt that the neo-black elite would prefer that government money come through some organization designated and approved by them.

In the end financial reparations would have the same effect as that of the various corporate/neo-black-elite alliances. It would serve to maintain an illusory power for the neo-black elite and the subjugation of the black masses.

A possible exception to this is the reparation proposal that came out of the National Black Economic Development Conference held in Detroit. The conference's participants, who represented some of today's more radical black spokesmen, attempted to come to grips with the entire question of black economic survival. The conference opposed the Nixon administration scheme for black capitalism. After demanding $500 million from white churches and Jewish synagogues in reparation for their part in the exploitation of black people, the conference went on record in support of the following ten-point program:

1. The establishment of a Southern Land Bank: $200 million.
2. The establishment of four major publishing and printing industries in the United States: $10 million each.
3. The establishment of four advanced scientific audio-visual networks to be located in Detroit, Cleveland, Chicago, and Washington, D.C.: $10 million each.
4. A research center which will provide information on the problems of black people: $30 million.
5. The establishment of a training center for the teaching of skills in community organization, photography, movie-making, television-making and repair, radio-building and repair, and all other skills needed in communication : $10 million.
6. Assistance in the organization of welfare recipients: $10 million.
7. The establishment of a National Labor Strike and Defense Fund: $20 million.
8. The establishment of an International Black Appeal: $20 million.
9. The establishment of a black university: $130 million.
10. All unused funds for the implementation of these demands.

The danger here, as in the other programs for reparations, is that it still has not been clearly stated just who will handle these funds and how they will be distributed or invested. Nonetheless, the conference's program is basically sound and does speak directly to the major needs of black people.

The other aspect of the reparations question is the demand for separate land. The black demand for land in America goes back at least to the late nineteenth century when an attempt was made by Edwin P. McCabe (in 1889) to petition the government to turn the land in the then Oklahoma Territory over to black people. McCabe intended to establish an all-black state with himself as governor.

The question of separate land for black people has since then been an important concern in the programs of many of the latter-day black separatist movements. (The best known of course is the Nation's.) The motivation behind the demand for land reparations, like that of financial reparations, is the desire to develop an independent black economy. The question of land is a question that has yet to be resolved in the minds of many in the separatist wing of today's neo-black elite. The disconcerting fact remains that a black group demanding separate land is still placing itself in a position of dependency. The black separatist feeling shared by many is entirely understandable. Integration is an issue that has never really had much relevancy to the immediate needs of black people. This, coupled with the recognition that the whole concept of integration was designed with only the most qualified black professional in mind, has more or less killed even the rhetoric of the "civil rights" movement today.

American Marxism, on the other hand, has in the past tended to bog down in its own verbiage and in general has failed to deal adequately with the problems confronting black workers. It seems that through the early history of Marxism in America, white Marxists have been just that: white first, and then—if anything remained of their ideals about the application of political ideology—Marxists. What has been desperately needed is a programmatic Marxist approach to solving the problems of black workers, instead of the thinly veiled unconscious (and not so unconscious) racism that has colored much of the working relationship white Communists have had with black people. So in this light, separatism has appealed to many in the black communities precisely because black people see no other way out of the oppression with which they are daily faced in America.

The neo-black elite has been able to play on this feeling. In doing so, they themselves haven't progressed past the point of thinking in terms of outdated capitalist economics as the basis for their future planning. This comes, however, at a time when the idea of a black separate nation on the same lines as the politico-economic structure of the United States runs counter to the new demands that a changing world is making on the systems of the West. There is also the question of how black people, not allowed to control their own communities in America, would be able to control a nation. A nation at this point is, in many ways, just as open to the types of economic-political subversion in which U.S. imperialism specializes as are the black communities inside the United States. Lenin clearly recognized the nature of capitalist subversion when he wrote: "Finance capital, in its drive to expand, can 'freely' buy or bribe the freest democratic or republican government and the elective officials of any, even an 'independent country.'"[4]

Black capitalism would in fact have very little chance of surviving in a separate land, within or without the United States. If this is not believed by the neo-black elite, they have only to look at the examples of many of the newly emergent Asian-African nations. Even the most superficial view would fully reveal the almost insurmountable difficulties a separate black nation in the United States would face in developing an independent economy. All the countries of Asia and Africa that have won their independence are visibly in possession of their own courts, legislative bodies, national leaders, and nearly every other facet of their national infrastructure. Yet these countries, with the possible exceptions of the People's Republic of China, and the republics of Guinea, Tanzania, Vietnam, and Korea, are economically subservient and politically controlled from the outside in the exact manner which Lenin described. United States imperialism has ruled out the possibility of international coexistence on the basis of economic and political give-and-take.

Even the countries mentioned as possible exceptions are

locked up in a death struggle with U.S. imperialism for their day-to-day survival. Take Guinea and Tanzania as examples. Here are two leading nations in Africa that have made some limited attempts to develop their national economies along socialistic lines. Even so, Guinea has had to rely on a Western consortium, Fria, which is strongly backed by American capital, to process its bauxite. In Tanzania, several United States firms, including the giant Anglo-American Corporation, are heavily involved in that country's mining, industrial, and financial operations. Cuba, in Latin America, is another example. Under Castro's leadership, Cuba has made enormous strides toward implementing socialism. Cuba, nevertheless, is under heavy attack from U.S. imperialism. The United States has been able to maintain a tight blockade around Cuba, forcing many shortages of food and industrial materials vitally needed for development. At the present, the United States is even able to hold a military base right on Cuban soil, at Guantanamo Bay (which incidentally has deprived Cuba of one of the world's finest natural harbors). U.S. imperialism is such an omnipresent world force that if it is not able to gain subtle access to the control of a national economy, it is always prepared to fall back on outright force and violence to gain its objective.

Ghana, where U.S. moneyed interests collaborated with that country's national elite to oust Dr. Osagyfo Kwame Nkrumah, champion of Pan-Africanism and socialism, is one proof. Vietnam is, of course, another. As a consequence of U.S. imperialism's naked aggression against the Vietnamese people, such major American corporations as Johnson & Johnson, Chase Manhattan Bank, Standard Oil, and Bank of America are now able to expand their activities from other Asian nations into Vietnam. Further, the South Vietnamese national elite, which has assisted the United States militarily against the people, has obligingly issued economic guarantees to American investors, among which are three- to five-year tax exemptions, pre-investment surveys at half the normal cost, freedom of movement in the transfer of capital and profits, and, to top it off, a fifteen-year guarantee against nationalization.[5]

Thus, even if the neo-black elite were to gain its demands for a separate land in which to build a black nation, the likelihood of surviving the external pressures of U.S. imperialism are very slim. And even if survival were possible it would be on the most minimal level, placing the new black nation squarely in the ranks of other Third World neo-colonies of the United States.

There is, however, another point to be considered here, and that is the right of all nations and peoples to self-determination. Some elements in the neo-black elite have chosen to draw on some of the revolutionary writings of the major Marxist theoreticians in order to buttress their argument for separation and black nationhood.

It must be made very clear on this point that it has indeed been the practice of nearly every Marxist thinker from Marx through Mao Tse-tung to uphold the basic right of oppressed national minority groups to determine their own destiny. Political-geographic separation should in fact be defended by every true revolutionary socialist on the basis of its being a legitimate extension of the right of oppressed peoples to self-determination. But for the principle of self-determination and separation to be truly meaningful, U.S. imperialism must first be totally destroyed. As has become very clear, U.S. imperialism respects no national boundary or national rights.

The U.S. Communist Party's draft resolution of 1928 on "The Negro Question in the United States" attempted to deal with both aspects of the black-separation/self-determination issue. The resolution reads in part: "If it [referring to the Black Belt area of the South] desires to separate, it must be free to do so; but if it prefers to remain federated with the United States it must also be free to do that. This is the correct meaning of the idea of self-determination."

But the resolution goes on to caution: "The Communists will carry on propaganda among the working masses of the Negro population against separation, in order to convince them that it is much better and in the interest of the Negro nation for the Black Belt to be a free republic, where the Negro majority has complete right of self-determination but remains governmentally federated with the great proletarian republic of the United States."

It is here that the advocates of a black national economy both in and apart from the United States have floundered in their analysis. They have either misinterpreted or revised to suit their own ends the writings of Marx and Lenin on self-determination and the national question. Lenin on this subject did point out that separation and/or national autonomy could be fought for under capitalism. The example of Norway's secession from Sweden was his major point of reference. But he took pains to explain that the ultimate success of genuine national independence was directly contingent on the triumph of the world proletarian socialist revolution. According to Lenin: "Victorious socialism must necessarily establish a full democracy and, consequently, not only introduce full equality of nations but also realise the right of the oppressed nations to self-determination, i.e., the right to free political separation."[6]

Lenin clearly delineates the provision that socialism must first become a reality. Without that, self-determination will never become an accomplished fact. Today more than ever, the dominating tendencies of capitalism toward the world's working masses make the logic behind this stipulation by Lenin compelling.

The same principle applies also in the cases of the various black cultural-nationalist groups that are working toward black nationhood by trying to win municipal elections in the large urban areas of the North where black people are beginning to be a majority of the numerical population. There are numerous examples of cities and towns that are completely black in population and have their own mayors and town officials: Mound Bayou, Mississippi; Robbins, Illinois; Boley, Oklahoma are three. But as is readily apparent from traveling through these towns, black control and an all-black population have not benefited these places one bit. Why? Because U.S. imperialism has a variety of tactics at its disposal to see that these towns are kept economically backward. The power has been transferred from the city to the county or state governments, which are exclusively or predominantly white middle- or upper-class controlled. If the cities that are already all-black are controlled and manipulated, how then will it be possible for the black cultural-nationalists such as LeRoi Jones (later Amiri Baraka) and the United Brothers in Newark to keep the other cities, where black people are in the majority, from the same fate?

The claim to land is, therefore, basically in the same category as financial reparations, rebate plans, and cooperatives. They are hastily thought-out measures designed to benefit the segment of the neo-black elite that has proposed them. Their effect would be to weaken even more the position of the black masses, at a time when uniform programs for politico-economic reconstruction in the black community are urgently needed.

5

And What of Africa?

Africa cannot accept the organic extension of any political or ideological system that does not respect its personality, its civilization, and its proper structure. . . . There is no demand other than that its people have the right to life and to possession of their land, their sun, their sky, and to free utilization and free disposal of their goods.

—SÉKOU TOURÉ

We are now entering a new phase. It is the phase of the second scramble for Africa. And just as in the first one tribe was divided against another tribe to make the division of Africa easier, in the second the technique will be to try to divide one nation against another nation, to make it easier to control Africa by making her weak and divided against herself.

—JULIUS K. NYERERE

I t is to be hoped that at some point the leaders of the neo-black elite will take time from their busy pursuit of black capitalist economics to seriously examine for themselves the condition today of the "Western-oriented" African nations, where black capitalism is very much a reality.

The Berlin Congress of 1885 was convened by the European colonial powers for the purpose of officially dividing up the African continent into European political-economic spheres of influence. Although the United States participated in the Congress, this was not the starting point for American economic involvement in Africa. For more than fifty years prior to the Berlin Congress, the United States had exercised a hegemony, tacitly recognized by the European powers, over key sections of West Africa. The initial American penetration in this part of Africa came with the settlement of Liberia in 1822.

The quasi-official American Colonization Society opened up Liberia with fifty-nine black people from the United States. The original intention of the Society was, with the cooperation of the American government, to use Liberia as a dumping ground for both the free black people of the North and any emancipated slaves in the South. However, a few in the Society felt that the hotly debated issue of black resettlement could serve as the perfect pretext for gaining a colonial base within Africa. The United States, under President Monroe, had already begun to view Latin America as a potential area for economic exploitation. So, it was concluded, why not Africa too?

Liberia, from its very beginning, was thoroughly American in everything from language to economics. The comparatively few black people who chose to emigrate from America to Liberia carried with them the customs, habits, and mannerisms they had learned from the white slave masters. It was noted that, within a short period of time, the American black settlers were trying to subjugate the indigenous African tribal people. As Carter G. Woodson, black historian and scholar, describes the situation: "Unfortunately those in control took their cue for the treatment of the natives from the slaveholders of the United States by whom their forebears were ... sent to [America]."[1]

For a few trinkets and some liquor paid to several African kings, the United States acquired both 43,000 acres of mineral-rich land and a *handpicked black elite to administer and develop that land.*

In 1847, Liberia was declared an independent nation. As one would expect, the political structure of the country was completely patterned after that of the United States. The constitution of Liberia was even drawn up by a Harvard Law School professor. The capital was "appropriately" named Monrovia in honor of Monroe. The Liberian national elite had, by now, swiftly moved toward concentrating its pitiable wealth and power into distinct class privilege.

Throughout every second of Liberia's early history, American businessmen and speculators had played some role in the internal affairs of the country. With the twentieth-century rise of American corporate power, Liberia became more and more dependent on the United States for its survival. Elihu Root, then Secretary of State, declared in 1908: "Liberia is an American colony." He went on to serve notice that the United States would conduct all the affairs of Liberia. In 1915, when the Liberian government was faced with a small-scale revolt against its oppressive policies by the Kroo tribe, the United States intervened militarily, dispatching the warship *Chester* to Monrovia. Following this, the Liberian government agreed to turn over to the U.S. War Department complete charge of the country's public defense. In 1924, $120,000 was spent on arming and training Liberia's security force. Interestingly enough, the United States saw fit to send its highest-ranking black army officer, Colonel Charles Young, to Liberia as a military adviser to the government there.

Facing financial collapse, the Liberian government in 1912 was forced to secure an international loan of $1,700,000, which was conveniently arranged by American bankers.[2] During World War I, the United States finally stepped in and took full management control of the Liberian economy. This move on the part of the United States paved the way for Firestone Rubber Company to enter Liberia.

In 1926, Firestone concluded an "agreement" with the Liberian government. By its terms, Firestone was allowed to set up a plantation on a million acres of government land for a term of ninety-nine years! As if this wasn't enough, the land was to be of Firestone's choosing where, and when, it got ready to expand. And what was required in return? Firestone, the agreement concluded, would pay the Liberian government a rental fee of six cents an acre! Adding insult to injury, Firestone was given the exclusive right to determine everything from the wages of its workers to what was to be grown on the land. Any minerals found on the land would belong to the company. The government of Liberia promised to supply Firestone with the workers necessary for them to exploit the land.[3] And, in 1926, the Liberian government established a labor bureau to secure the necessary labor for the Firestone plantation. For each worker the bureau found, the government was paid one cent a day.

Astounding is the word here, for what this amounted to was that Firestone was simply being given land by the American government, with their political stooges, the Liberian government, looking on. It was a case of U.S. imperialism in its boldest form.

In another part of the "agreement," Firestone extended a loan to the Liberian government which supposedly enabled the government to cover most of the debts it had incurred. The loan itself was in the neighborhood of $5 million at an interest rate of 7 percent.[4] The usurious rate of interest demanded by Firestone should not come as a surprise to anyone familiar with the role played by American corporate capitalism in the Third World. Traditionally, high rates of interest and short-term repayment provisions on loans are tactical devices employed by the Western nations in their overall plans for economic subversion and control of the Third World.

This presents a stark contrast to the policy of the socialist countries. It is common knowledge that most loans from socialist countries are extended on a long-term basis, with flexible provisions for repayment. Most important, these loans are usually at a minimal rate of interest (around 2.5 percent) as compared with the exorbitant interest rates (5 to 10 percent) demanded on loans from the Western capitalist nations. Firestone, then, is by no means atypical.

Liberia today could correctly be characterized as a colonial appendage of Firestone Rubber Co. Firestone has so completely dominated the Liberian national economy over the last forty years that it has even been able to create auxiliary government positions and disband others. Firestone has been so vicious in its dealings with Liberia that at one point the old League of Nations, certainly no friend of the colonial peoples of the Third World, was forced to conduct investigations into its practices.

From the early 1940s up until 1965, Firestone extracted a supply of rubber from Liberia worth $160 million. The Liberian government in return has received from Firestone a net $8 million![5] It has been estimated that Firestone's profits have amounted to three times the Liberian government's total revenues from all sources.[6]

And what of the Liberian national elite, the black capitalists of Liberia? Apparently, they are satisfied with their relations with Firestone. William Tubman, leader of the elite and president of Liberia for twenty-four years, has set out to make the Liberian capital a showplace for American capitalism in West Africa. Tubman himself reportedly lives in a luxurious million-dollar palace. Such conspicuous consumption, an acknowledged by-product of American economic influence, is commonplace with the elite in Liberia, as it is throughout all the other Western-oriented elite-controlled African nations. Alongside this, the average per capita income of the Liberian worker is $150 a year. The Liberian elite, propped up by Firestone to protect its interests, has assigned itself much of the salaried income in the country, while the workers and peasants survive on a subsistence level, if that.

George Padmore, in his discussion of Liberia, had this to say: "The situation in Liberia . . . shows that Negro capitalists will oppress and exploit other Negroes, just as the whites do, when they are in the economic position to do so." Little in the way of further analysis is necessary: the point has been made, and the obvious parallel demands that one draw the obvious conclusion. As for the rest of Africa, the pattern that has prevailed in Liberia is apparent today over nearly the entire continent. The average annual per capita income in the nearly fifty "independent" nations and territories on the African continent is roughly $250.[7] The only exception to this is white, American-backed, racist-ruled South Africa, where the per capita income exceeds $400. Nearly one-third of these African countries have an annual per capita income of less than $80. This makes the workers of Africa, along with those of Asia, the most economically impoverished group of people in the world.[8]

African workers are faced with circumstances similar to those faced by black workers in the United States. And cultural differences notwithstanding, the national elites in African countries are in almost the same position as the black elite in the United States. All are being encouraged to follow the capitalist economic line; in the case of the African elites, this has occurred on the national level, while with the American black elite it has occurred on the local community level. In many cases some of the very same corporations which are operating in both Africa and black America are the busiest in promoting black capitalism. The Rockefeller Foundation, which has direct ties to David Rockefeller's Chase Manhattan Bank—one of South Africa's biggest investors—and U.S. Steel are two notable examples. The Rockefeller Foundation is at present intimately involved in the Urban Coalition, a make-shift group of corporate businessmen, public officials, and "civil rights leaders" that is hard at work trying to develop black business potential in black America.

U.S. Steel is busy with a similar program in the black community in Pittsburgh. At the same time, U.S. Steel, through its French subsidiary, COMILOG, controls the rich manganese ore deposits of the Gabon Republic. As a result, U.S. Steel has become one of the chief economic influences in the Gabon economy. And of course, Rockefeller interests are spread all over Africa.[9]

The African worker, like the black worker in America, is a

victim of an American corporate-controlled elite whose main "accomplishment" has been to force upon him all the negative tendencies toward class polarization.

The national ruling elite in each of the impoverished African nations is gradually being transformed into a Pan-African elite, whose sole interest is the complete domination of every facet of African life.

A recognizable characteristic of this new Pan-African elite, outside of the members' common miseducation in Western universities, has been the close relations they have maintained with their respective countries' armies. Tight control is an absolute necessity to them. The officers in their armies have also been trained mostly in Western universities and military schools. Sol Dubula, in the *African Communist* (first quarter, 1967), provides a very interesting analysis of the role of England's Sandhurst in the training and development of many of the newly "independent" African nations' army officers. It was noted here that the leading officers in the Ghanaian army, which engineered the coup overthrowing the Nkrumah government, were trained at Sandhurst. These same officers today comprise the ruling military junta (another form of the elite) in Ghana. To top it all off, they have chosen to call themselves the National Liberation Council.

Colonel A. A. Afrifa, a member of the Council, is an example of a product of the type of Western-brainwashed training that Sandhurst is noted for. Colonel Afrifa wrote a book in which he glowingly depicted his years at Sandhurst. In regard to Britain and the Commonwealth, Afrifa has written:

> I have been trained in the United Kingdom as a soldier, and I am ever prepared to fight alongside my friends in the United Kingdom in the same way as Canadians and Australians will do. How could we be friends belonging to the Commonwealth and stay out in time of Commonwealth adversity, and when this great Union is in danger?[10]

Replace the words "United Kingdom" and "Commonwealth" in the above quote, and these words could easily be mistaken for the words that have been uttered by the black captains and majors in the U.S. Army. Both are members of their elites (black and Pan-African). And both are equally good examples of how well Western imperialism has done its job!

It has done its job so well that at the moment American corporate enterprise dominates the national economies of many other African states. In several cases, the profits extracted yearly by a few of the major corporate firms total more than the entire revenue of some of these governments combined. In some of the smaller African nations, a single American corporation has, at given times, made up nearly the entire economy of the country in which it was operating.

A look at the figures on American corporate investment in Africa reveals just how deeply imperialism has embedded itself in the economic fabric of Africa. In the period from 1945 to 1958, American corporate investment in Africa increased from $110 million to $789 million. Most of this investment was drawn from profits. Overall American profits, including reinvestment of surpluses, were estimated at $704 million. At the same time the net loss to African countries during this period was $555 million. The gross profit for all American corporations during this same period has been placed by some estimates at $1.5 million (official U.S. government figures claimed the amount of profit was $1.234 million).[11]

This period marked the first really large-scale American economic expansion into Third World nations. To do this, the United States skillfully used the alleged "Cold War" and "international communism." Thus it was able to open up new areas, such as Southeast Asia and the Middle East, for economic exploitation. The results can be readily seen in Africa today. According to official government figures, the U.S. income from both government and corporate investment in Asia and Africa (excluding South Africa) in 1967 was placed at nearly $2 billion. The trend, despite the liberation wars being waged, is very much upward. In the first quarter of 1968, income on government-corporate investments was up $35 million over the last quarter of 1967.[12]

When considering these figures, it is important to keep in mind that much of Africa before 1960 was still governed on a colonial basis by European nations, whereas after 1960 most of the African nations in the United Nations had gained their "political independence." It has been in this short space of only eight years that American corporate enterprise has made its greatest economic gains on the African continent. The obvious conclusion to draw from this fact is that the formal "independence" of African nations from Europe has been *a tremendous boon to American corporate enterprise.* The United States has stepped in and filled every economic power vacuum left by the departing European colonial masters. It can honestly be stated that U.S. corporate power has now penetrated the Third World economically on a scale that would have made the British colonial office at the height of its power feel envious.

Kenya, under the rule of Jomo Kenyatta, provides an instructive example in black capitalism. Kenyatta, it was felt by the masses of Kenyan workers and peasants, would be the ideal person to lead the newly "independent" Kenyan nation out of the economic morass in which British colonial rule had trapped it. However, it has now become apparent to many of the Kenyan people that Kenyatta was never the strong nationalist figure that he appeared to be before "independence."

The explanation is simple. Kenyatta, even when he was supposedly defying the British during colonialism, still retained his allegiance, not to mention his identification, with Britain. Kenyatta, needless to say, is one of the leading figures in the Pan-African elite. So it is not surprising to find that U.S. imperialism is at present making a strong bid for control of the Kenyan economy. As of August 1967, there were some sixty-seven American corporate firms (represented by agencies) operating in Kenya. The total investment for these firms was $100 million. In June

1965, the Kenyan government instituted exchange control, supposedly a countermeasure, which was designed to cut down the profits the Western corporate firms were taking out of the country. But this was strictly a facade. The corporations operating in Kenya would never tolerate any real move to check their exploitative designs. So the Kenyan elite instituted, and note this well, a "special act of Parliament" that "protected" all foreign investments in Kenya, by giving them "approved enterprise status." All this means, then, is that the corporate firms doing business in Kenya are allowed to keep on exploiting the Kenyan people. This is yet another example of how imperialism and the Pan-African elite work together in their co-partnership in black capitalism.

Frantz Fanon, in his revolutionary study, *The Wretched of the Earth*, sums up quite well the general character of the Pan-African elite:

As it [the Pan-African elite] does not share its profits with the people, and in no way allows them to enjoy any of the dues that are paid to it by the foreign companies, it will discover the need for a popular leader to whom will fall the dual role of stabilising the regime and of perpetuating the domination of the bourgeoisie.

The people who for years on end have seen this leader and heard him speak, who from a distance in a kind of a dream have followed his contests with the colonial power, spontaneously put their trust in this patriot. Before independence, the leader generally embodies the aspirations of the people for independence, political liberty and national dignity. But as soon as independence is declared, far from embodying in concrete form the needs of the people in what touches bread, land and the restoration of the country to the sacred hands of the people, the leader will reveal his true inner purpose: to become the general president of that company of profiteers impatient for their returns which constitutes the national bourgeoisie.[13]

Which are these American corporations that are so involved in the control of the African continent? The list reads like a register of blue-chip corporations. Many, as mentioned before, have reputations for their "generous and enthusiastic support" for "civil rights" for black people in America. Some examples are: the banking and finance institutions of Rockefeller and Morgan, Dillon Read, U.S. Steel, Union Carbide, Alcoa, Kaiser, and Bethlehem Steel. Much of the rubber of West Africa is still controlled by Firestone, with B. F. Goodrich coming on fast.

In fact, everything from the diamond and gold mines of Central and South Africa, to the oil wells of North Africa, to the bauxite, cocoa, peanuts, and coffee of West Africa, to the cotton of East Africa, is exploited by private American corporations for their own profit.

Along with this white-imperialist-controlled black capitalism in Africa, there is the white capitalism of South Africa. It is still United States corporate capitalism that furnishes what is perhaps the prime economic and military support for the white killer governments in southern Africa. When the South African government was faced with economic instability in 1960–61, after it massacred black people at Sharpeville, the Rockefeller Chase Manhattan Bank advanced a $10 million loan to save the government. Other American investors, who apparently did not want to be identified, put up a $70 million loan to the government.[14] Another consortium of American banks, which includes such stalwarts of American finance as the Bank of America and Morgan Guaranty Trust, made available to South Africa a revolving credit fund of $50 million.[15]

Since then, the number of American corporate investors in South Africa has tripled. Kennecott Copper, Anglo American, Englehard Industries (whose president, Charles Englehard, is one of the Democratic Party's biggest boosters), Chrysler Corp., Ford Motors, Pan-American Airways, Singer Sewing Machine Co., and Mobil Oil—to mention a few—are some of the corporations involved in the grab bag. By 1965, American economic investment in South Africa had climbed to $467 million.[16] The overall rate of return on American economic investment was almost 20 percent, or $87 million, in 1965.

And what of the African worker in South Africa? The South African white has the highest standard of income in Africa. This is the only reason why South Africa has the highest per capita income of any country in Africa. The black African worker, in contrast, has an average annual income of around $150. The only exceptions are the mineworkers, because mining is the most prosperous sector of the South African economy. But even here there has been a decline, for while in 1935 the average annual income of a black mineworker was $203, by 1960 it was only $196. Meanwhile, the average annual income for a white mineworker has risen a thousand dollars in the same period, to $3,214.[17]

An average of $200 a year is spent on the education of a white student while $20 is spent on the black student. Ninety percent of the most fertile and productive land is in the hands of the white settlers, while the remainder of the land is subsisted on by over 12 million blacks.

The final question is, where does the U.S. government, defender of the principle of self-determination, stand on this issue? As Carl Oglesby points out:

> Publicly, our government deplores Afrikaaner racism . . . and is no doubt appalled to know that poison gases—soman, sarin and tabun—are being manufactured in large doses in South Africa. But embargo or not, the South African armed forces fly in 36 F-86 Sabrejet interceptors . . . C-47 and C-130B transports . . . and about 30 Sikorsky helicopters.[18]

All of these armaments are American.

Finally, American corporate enterprise and the Pan-African elite at present comprise a pivotal power-axis on which the political-economic control of Africa hinges. Regrettably, it appears that this alliance will remain intact as long as the Pan-African elite can convince the masses of African workers that the African brand of bourgeois democracy is working in their interests, at the same time, of course, hiding the truth from them about African socialism —which represents genuine working-class democracy. At this point, the two factions have the situation so locked up that only a few countries in Africa (Guinea, Tanzania, Algeria, Mali, and the United Arab Republic) have even been able to adopt socialism as their stated goal.

I have purposely chosen to draw out the foregoing facts concerning present-day Africa for I feel that Africa serves as the perfect model for black capitalism in actual practice. Nearly all of the African nations that have gained "independence" are today trapped in a neo-colonialist swamp precisely because of their ties to the economies of the former European mother countries. Black capitalism on the African continent must share the blame for this. In Africa, the black business class of each nation has reserved for itself many of the comforts previously enjoyed by the European colonists. In every major African city from Dakar to Nairobi the same townhouses, yachts, exquisite food, and elegant clothes enrich the life of this new clique. This is of course a situation comparable to that beginning to develop among America's black elite.

Alongside this, there is that movement of corporate enterprise that is comparable in Africa to that in America. For example, corporations like Shell, Standard Oil, and Coca-Cola that are active in African exploitation were well represented at a black business fair (Black Expo '69) held in Chicago in October. As should be apparent, the pursuit of black capitalism, whether in Africa or America, entails a great deal of danger. At some point in the African masses' drive for true liberation there will be a confrontation with the Pan-African elite. The conflict of interest between them may prove too great to be resolved peacefully. One might also expect a similar kind of clash between the masses of blacks in America, who are overwhelmingly working class, and the black elite. Black capitalism in Africa, America, or anywhere else is in basic conflict with the rising aspirations of oppressed people. It is clear that if the black elite in America hopes to avoid the same kind of conflict that is coming in Africa they will have to move away from blind adherence to the Western precepts of economic development.

Conclusion

In every part of America, the black elite is increasing its efforts in the area of capitalist economics. This is readily apparent from a brief rundown of recent developments in the following major cities:

In Cleveland, three black development firms—the McKinney Plumbing Co., Namax Builders, Inc., and the Richardson Electric Co.—have all received aid from such corporate interests as the U.S. Gypsum Co., the Ford Foundation, and the Catholic Diocese of Cleveland for various "redevelopment projects" within Cleveland's black community.

In Boston, Sanders Associates, a black subsidiary firm of Eastern Gas and Fuel Co., was formed to share in the building of 3,200 housing units. For this Eastern Gas received a $32 million contract from the FHA and the Boston Rehabilitation Corporation. Also, in June, the black-owned Unity Bank was opened in Boston's Roxbury district. Big banking interests such as the Boston National Shawmut Bank and the New England Merchants National Bank helped Unity in its planning. After six months, Unity's president, Donald Sneed, a black real estate broker, reported a profit of $47,520.

In Baltimore, small black merchants were selected by B. Green and Co., a major grocery wholesaler, as outlets for its large-scale ghetto food-marketing business.

In Los Angeles, the Green Power Foundation, originally organized by several local black businessmen to produce the "Watts Walloper" baseball bat, has recently branched out into other areas of production. It now operates a small trucking company, a gas station, and a factory which produces a variety of woodcraft items ranging from furniture to picnic tables. Also, the Sons of Watts, a black youth group, has signed a lease agreement to operate a Standard Oil gas station in the Watts area.

In Philadelphia, eight of that city's largest banks have formed a Job Loan Corporation responsible for administering a $3 million loan-guarantee program for black businesses.

In Columbus, Georgia, Mainstream Inc. was formed by a group of black businessmen for the purpose of seeking marketing franchises for blacks interested in business.

In Houston, twenty-three banks have combined to offer a $7 million loan fund for the promotion and establishment of black businesses.

In San Francisco, twenty-five black business investors led by Charles Bussey, operator of a furniture-restoring firm, formed the San Francisco Container Corp. The Bank of America and the Fireman's Fund Insurance Co. loaned the Corporation $180,000 to get them off the ground. In another development, several black investors led by James Brown, the noted soul singer, have formed a trading-stamp concern known as the Black & Brown Trading Stamp Corp. Such a business, according to Donald Warden, attorney and chairman of the corporation's board, "is enlightened black capitalism."

In Rochester, New York, the Rochester Business Opportunities Corp., controlled primarily by Eastman Kodak, has set up a program aimed at the organization of black businesses. To date, RBOC has helped some twenty-four blacks open up businesses. In a similar move, Xerox has been working with FIGHT, a so-called black militant organization, to establish a black-owned company for the manufacture of transformers and metal stampings.

In Kansas City, Missouri, a group of local black businessmen have joined together to open a million-dollar printing company known as Lithon Color Press, Inc. Also, within the past year a new black bank, the Swope Parkway National Bank, was founded there.

In Seattle, Washington, several black investors recently opened the Liberty Bank.

In Chicago, the Blackstone Rangers, a black street gang, recently announced the opening of their service station-car wash, formerly operated by the Humble Oil Co. The Rangers are already operating a restaurant. In this respect it is interesting to note that two leading Ranger members attended Nixon's inaugural ball at his personal invitation. Apparently in appreciation, the Rangers returned the favor by inviting Nixon to their car-wash opening. Also, Operation Breadbasket, an adjunct of SCLC, has won, after an extended boycott, an agreement from the A&P grocery store chain to sell the products made by twenty-five black businesses. A&P has also agreed to market the products of five black suppliers throughout its entire 260-store chain.

The above outline of recent happenings in the field of black business development indicates that corporate enterprise and the black elite have teamed up to implement their designs on a national scale. The black elite, in addition to its already concrete plans for ghetto domination, has devised other schemes to effect its goals. The recently proposed Booker T. Washington Fund is a good example. The Booker T. Washington Fund, the brainchild of the National Business League, is presented as a non-profit black corporation which will exist for the purpose of increasing the number of black businesses. The NBL seeks to finance the fund through the contributions of various large corporations in America. As Berkeley Burrell, president of the NBL, has put it: "The NBL proposes that the famed 'Fortune 500' corporations start the Fund along its way with a contribution of $10,000 each. The next 1,000 firms going down the scale in size should contribute $5,000. Every good-sized firm in the nation should contribute at least $1,000, and no business in the country should fail to contribute something to this economic growth seed-fund."

This is, of course, only one example of the black elite's push. Other members of the black community are being actively pursued by the black elite and urged to join in the "new" program for "black liberation." Well-known black athletes, entertainers, and socialites have been swept up by the ideas of business. For instance, James Brown, in addition to the trading-stamp company mentioned above, has numerous other business investments, including: two radio stations, a production office, a record company, and various real estate interests. Brown is of course a multimillionaire. He plans to invest part of his estimated $3 million gross income into four more radio stations and a chain of black-managed restaurants.

Muhammad Ali is another case. Ali was recently in the forefront of the planning to establish a chain of drive-in restaurants. Since then several "Champburger" restaurants have opened. For the use of his image and name, Ali has received 6 percent of the Champburger Corporation's stock. Ali will also receive royalties of 1 percent of the business's annual net sales.

Corporate capitalism's politicians have also gotten into the act in recent weeks. Spiro Agnew, for one, issued a forthright endorsement of the black elite's plans when he said in an April 1969 speech: "When that lone black businessman walks into a bank, let it be a bank run by a black man. Let him have the collateral assistance we have. Let him have the same public relations we have, led by a black man to sell his product on competitive markets like we do."

While Agnew was saying these words his President, Richard Nixon, was busy signing into law the executive order that created the Office of Minority Business Enterprise. This measure is seen by Nixon as a means of implementing his program for black entrepreneurship.

At the same time, Congress is considering a CORE-endorsed Community Self-Determination Act. This Act was originally introduced into Congress last July under the bipartisan sponsorship of thirty-five Senators. It calls for the institution of Community Development Corporations within local black communities. It has not been widely understood, but these corporations will not be controlled in any collective way by the communities themselves. Rather, the corporations will be financed by Community Development Banks also established by the Act. To obtain capital the banks will sell stock to the CDC's and to private corporate investors. This neat arrangement will ensure that both the community corporations and the banks will be controlled by the outside white business interests. Even worse, corporate business investors will be guaranteed a sizable profit because an assortment of tax benefits, as stipulated under the provisions of the Act, will be afforded to the CDC's business operations. According to the tax-privilege provisions of the Act, the Internal Revenue Code would be amended to make possible a sliding scale for surtax exemption, based on local unemployment and income levels; greater corporate surtax exemptions for subsidiaries of a CDC; and 100 percent deduction from the gross income of a parent CDC of dividends passed on to it from subsidiaries (it has been estimated that the normal rate here is 85 percent).

The Small Business Administration has also stepped up its activities in the area of ghetto business promotion. In Los Angeles, for example, the SBA has just initiated a Minority Entrepreneurship Program (popularly referred to as Project OWN). Alvin Meyers, regional SBA director, says that Project OWN, with proper SBA direction, will enable minority business-men to either establish new businesses or buy out white owners of old ones. Project OWN will extend both direct loans or bank loans guaranteed up to 90 percent by the SBA to the prospective businessmen.

Meyers has also revealed that the SBA in Los Angeles granted sixty-seven loans to minority businessmen, totalling $1,867,000, in the six-month period ending December 31, 1968. According to Meyers, this number exceeded the number of minority loans extended for the entire 1967–68 fiscal year (sixty-two loans totalling $1,304,000).

Nonetheless, all blacks are not fooled by these developments. Organized resistance to the empty cries for black capitalism is on the rise. What is significant about the resistance being mounted by many blacks is that there is a historical precedent.

About fifty years ago, Cyril V. Briggs, a black leader, founded an organization known as the African Blood Brotherhood. The Brotherhood was an all-black organization dedicated to the struggle for black liberation. The Brotherhood adopted an eight-point program which was far and away the most radical program of the day. In fact the program of the Brotherhood anticipated many of the actions and events occurring today in the black communities. For our purposes, though, let us take note of the contemporary relevance of point one of the Brotherhood's program: "A liberated race—in the United States, Africa, and elsewhere. Liberated not merely from political rule, but also from the crushing weight of capitalism, which keeps the many in degrading poverty that the few may wallow in stolen wealth." [1]

By the same token, anyone involved today in the developing liberation struggle in the United States should, like Briggs, be searching for and thinking about ways through which black and white workers can benefit fully from the fruits of their labor. This would be better than trying to make a system work for black workers which has not even worked for many white workers.

Black people, it is true, have been carefully fed on myths and illusions for many years now, and the popularity of the demand for black capitalism is, one might say, the culminating result.

That many so-called black leaders should waste black people's valuable time and energy chasing another of the American ruling class's myths is understandable *but it is inexcusable.* For black Americans have the opportunity today as never before to learn

from the experiences of the many sincere genuine revolutionary people throughout the world. These are the people who are
trying to build a way for development. However, as a means of
raising black national consciousness, such an effort is sound.
Even more, it opens up fresh possibilities for cementing broader
tactical coalitions with other oppressed groups around common,
related issues such as the draft, the Vietnam War, strikes, etc.

Only when state political power is genuinely in the hands of an
aroused and conscious American people, and economic imperialism is ended, will the liberation struggles of black and Third
World peoples be fully successful. For it is an acknowledged fact
that the United States now occupies the odious position of being
the center of world reaction.

The struggle of the black masses for liberation will spur other
oppressed people to fight for their liberation; it already has. Black
capitalism certainly has no place in this struggle.

ALL POWER TO THE PEOPLE

Bibliography

Carmichael, Stokely, and Hamilton, Charles V. *Black Power: The Politics of
    Liberation in America.* New York: Random House, 1967.
Cruse, Harold. *Rebellion or Revolution?* New York: William Morrow, 1968.
Delaney, M. R., and Campbell, Robert. *Search for a Place: Black Separatism and
    Africa, 1860.* Ann Arbor: University of Michigan Press, 1969.
Dobb, Maurice. *Economic Growth and Underdeveloped Countries.* New York:
    International Publishers, 1963.
Domhoff, G. William. *Who Rules America?* Englewood Cliffs, New Jersey:
    Prentice-Hall, 1967.
Du Bois, W. E. B. *The Philadelphia Negro.* New York: Schocken, 1967.
Fanon, Frantz. *The Wretched of the Earth.* New York: Grove Press, 1963.
Frazier, E. Franklin. *Black Bourgeoisie.* New York: Collier, 1962.
Frazier, E. Franklin. *The Negro in the United States.* New York: Macmillan, 1957.
Franklin, John Hope. *From Slavery to Freedom.* New York: Vintage, 1969.
Essien-Udom, E. U. *Black Nationalism.* New York: Dell Publishing, 1962.
Garvey, Marcus. *Philosophy and Opinions.* San Francisco: Julian Richardson
    Associates, 1967.
Jalée, Pierre. *The Pillage of the Third World.* New York: Monthly Review Press,
    1968.
Lenin, V. I. *National Liberation, Socialism and Imperialism*, in *Selected
    Writings.* New York: International Publishers, 1968.
Lenin, V. I. *Imperialism: The Highest Stage of Capitalism.* New York:
    International Publishers, 1939.
Thornbrough, E. L., ed. *Booker T. Washington.* Englewood Cliffs, New Jersey:
    Prentice-Hall, 1969.

Notes

Introduction to the First Edition

1. E. Franklin Frazier, *Black Bourgeoisie* (New York: Collier Books, 1957), p. 139.

1. The Origin of the Legacy

1. W. E. B. Du Bois, *The World and Africa* (New York: International Publishers, 1946), p. 163.
2. Melville J. Herskovits, *The Myth of the Negro Past* (Boston: Beacon Press, 1941), pp. 160–61.
3. E. Franklin Frazier, *The Negro in the United States* (New York: Macmillan, 1957), p. 369.
4. W. E. B. Du Bois, *The Philadelphia Negro* (New York: Schocken Books, 1967), p. 24.
5. Eugene Boykin, "Enterprise and Accumulation of Negroes Prior to 1860." Research done as part of master's thesis, Columbia University, 1932.
6. W. E. B. Du Bois, *The Philadelphia Negro,* p. 123.
7. Boykin, "Enterprise and Accumulation of Negroes."
8. Ibid.
9. Ibid.
10. Ibid.
11. Bill McAdoo, *Pre–Civil War Black Nationalism* (A Progressive Labor Party pamphlet), p. 13.
12. Ibid., p. 14.
13. Ibid., p. 10.
14. Ibid.
15. A. H. Stone, *Free Contract Labor in the South* (Building of the Nation series, vol. 5).

16. Frederick Douglass, *Life and Times of Frederick Douglass* (New York: Collier Books, 1962), p. 403.
17. Abram Harris, *The Negro as Capitalist: A Study of Banking and Business Among American Negroes* (College Park, MD: McGrath, 1969), p. 198.
18. Frazier, *The Negro in the United States*, p. 396.
19. Harris, *The Negro as Capitalist*, pp. 172-73.
20. Frazier, *Black Bourgeoisie*, p. 50.
21. Harris, *The Negro as Capitalist*, pp. 49-50.
22. Ibid., p. 393.
23. Herbert Aptheker, ed., *A Documentary History of the Negro People in the United States* (New York: Citadel Press, 1969), p. 847.
24. For more detailed discussion, see Frazier's *Black Bourgeoisie*, p. 133.
25. Benjamin Quarles, *The Negro American* (Glenview, IL: Scott, Foresman and Co., 1967), p. 346.
26. Edmund David Cronon, *Black Moses: The Story of Marcus Garvey and the Universal Negro Improvement Association* (Madison: University of Wisconsin Press, 1955), p. 16.
27. Ibid., p. 60.
28. Ibid., p. 196.
29. Harold Cruse, *The Crisis of the Negro Intellectual* (New York: William Morrow, 1967), p. 333.
30. Cronon, *Black Moses*, p. 59.
31. St. Clair Drake and Horace R. Cayton, *Black Metropolis* (New York: Harper & Row, 1962), vol. 2, p. 438.
32. Frazier, *Black Bourgeoisie*, pp. 50-51.
33. Frazier, *The Negro in the United States*, p. 407.
34. Ibid., p. 408.
35. Drake and Cayton, *Black Metropolis*, p. 461.
36. Ibid., p. 487.
37. Ibid.
38. Ibid., p. 479, Table 22.

2. Black Religion and Capitalism

1. Frazier, *Black Bourgeoisie*, p. 152.
2. Drake and Cayton, *Black Metropolis*, p. 431.
3. E. U. Essien-Udom, *Black Nationalism* (New York: Dell Publishing, 1962), p. 182.
4. Leo Huberman, "The Responsibility of the Socialist," in *Socialism Is the Only Answer* (Monthly Review Pamphlet Series: No. 3), p. 5.
5. *Recent Trends in Social and Economic Conditions of Negroes in the United States*, U.S. Department of Labor, Bureau of Labor Statistics, July 1968, p. 16.
6. Essien-Udom, *Black Nationalism*, p. 191.
7. Ibid., p. 286.
8. Ibid.

3. Whose Capitalism?

1. V. I. Lenin, *Imperialism: the Highest Stage of Capitalism* (Moscow: Progress Publishers, 1968), p. 15.
2. Richard Cloward and Frances Fox Piven, *The Nation,* October 16, 1967, p. 367.
3. *Muhammad Speaks,* October 11, 1968, p. 12.
4. *Liberator,* October 1968, editorial by Dan Watts.
5. Cloward and Piven, *The Nation,* p. 366.
6. For a complete listing of National Negro Business Associations in the United States, see: *A Guide to Negro Marketing Information,* U.S. Department of Commerce, September 1966, p. 27.
7. Eugene P. Foley, "The Negro Businessman: In Search of a Tradition," in *The Negro American,* ed. Talcott Parsons and Kenneth B. Clark (Boston: Beacon Press, 1967).
8. Ibid., p. 569. Foley also says: "The Negro, therefore, is hardly any further advanced in business today than he was in the 1820s" (p. 573).
9. Andrew Brimmer, Address at Atlanta University, March 1964. Department of Commerce press release, p. 2.
10. Harding Young, "Negro Participation in American Business," *Journal of Negro Education* 32 (Fall 1963), pp. 391–96.
11. *Muhammad Speaks,* September 27, 1968, p. 38, interview with Berkeley G. Burrell, president of the National Business League.
12. Bill McAdoo, *Notes on Black Liberation,* p. 9 of pamphlet reprint of an article that appeared in *Progressive Labor,* October 1965.
13. Frazier, *The Negro in the United States,* p. 410.
14. *Muhammad Speaks,* September 27, 1968, p. 33.
15. "A Negro Millionaire's Advice to His Race," *U.S. News & World Report,* September 4, 1967, p. 68.
16. Ibid.
17. Augustus Hawkins, "The Black Demand for Money Power," *Los Angeles Sentinel,* October 1968.

4. Black Capitalism's Other Faces

1. *Muhammad Speaks,* November 22, 1968, p. 38.
2. Frazier, *The Negro in the United States,* p. 409.
3. *Los Angeles Herald-Dispatch,* November 21, 1968, p. 1.
4. V. I. Lenin, "National Liberation, Socialism and Imperialism," in *Selected Writings* (New York: International Publishers, 1968), p. 112.
5. Victor Perlo, *The Vietnam Profiteers* (New York: New Outlook Publishers, 1966), pp. 16–17.
6. V. I. Lenin, *Selected Writings,* p. 10.

5. And What of Africa?

1. Bill McAdoo, *Pre-Civil War Black Nationalism,* p. 14.

2. R. Earle Anderson, *Liberia* (Chapel Hill: University of North Carolina Press, 1952), p. 93. The author of this work, despite his blatant racism, has inadvertently let out some important facts about the nature of U.S. imperialism's historic operation in Liberia.

3. Ibid., pp. 129–38.

4. Ibid., p. 94.

5. Kwame Nkrumah, *Neo-Colonialism: The Last Stage of Imperialism* (New York: International Publishers, 1965), p. 66.

6. Ibid.

7. Ibid. See table on per capita income, p. 5.

8. Ibid.

9. Ibid. Nkrumah presents a wealth of factual data and information on the operations of most of the Western corporations that are involved in the exploitation of Africa's resources. Note the chapter on "Monopoly Capitalism and the American Dollar," particularly. A reading of this will quickly reveal why Nkrumah was such a threat to U.S. imperialism.

10. Jack Woddis, *Introduction to Neo-Colonialism* (New York: International Publishers, 1967), p. 86.

11. Nkrumah, *Neo-Colonialism*, p. 62.

12. These statistics were taken from the *Survey of Current Business,* U.S. Department of Commerce (June 1968), vol. 48, no. 6.

13. Frantz Fanon, *The Wretched of the Earth* (New York: Grove Press, 1965), p. 134.

14. Carl Oglesby and Richard Shaull, *Containment and Change* (New York: Macmillan Company, 1967), p. 98.

15. Ibid., p. 99.

16. Ibid., p. 100.

17. Ibid.

18. Ibid., p. 101.

Conclusion

1 Theodore Draper, *American Communism and Soviet Russia* (New York: Viking Press, 1960), p. 325.

Index